NOW WASH YOUR HANDS!

NOW WASH
YOUR HANDS!

NOW WASH YOUR HANDS!

*More than you ever
wanted to know
about the life and times
of the toilet*

STEPHEN ARNOTT

PRION

First published 2001 by
Prion Books Limited
Imperial Works, Perren Street,
London NW5 3ED
www.prionbooks.com

ISBN-1-85375-453-6

A catalogue record of this book can be obtained from the
British Library

Printed and bound in Great Britain by
Creative Print & Design, Wales

Contents

Introduction   viii

History of the Toilet Part One   1
History of the Toilet Part Two   13
History of the Toilet Part Three   25
History of the Toilet Part Four   35
Going to the Loo   43
Cold Weather Crapping   63
Wiping Up   69
Chamber Pots   81
Urinals   93
Public Toilets   101
Cesspits   113
Composting Crappers   119
Transport Toilets   127

Military Loos	139
Loos in Space	153
Crappers of All Nations	159
Uses of Excrement	171
Holy Shit!	183
Customs and Superstitions	195
Rude Toilet Behaviour	205
Death on the Loo	215
Toilets, Humour and the Arts	223
Words and Phrases	237
References	00
Index	00

Introduction

In a survey conducted by a popular science magazine to find out what its readers considered to be the top 100 inventions of all time, beating all other contenders including fire, the computer, and the wheel, was the toilet.

This book is a tribute to that humble invention. Designed to help those curious about the world of the loo, it is a complete toilet reference, bringing the subject out of the (water) closet to tell you everything you ever wanted to know (and a few things you didn't) about the culture and practices of the smallest room in the house.

Now Wash Your Hands outlines the history of the toilet from the simple limestone lavatories of the Ancient Egyptians, through the garderobes of medieval Europe, the invention of the Elizabethan water closet, the glorious heyday of the Victorian crapper, and the final frontier of high-tech space commodes.

Different toilet types are also examined: the domestic privy, the army slit-trench, the sea-going yacht toilet, airline loos, the eco-friendly composting commode, the lowly chamber pot and many others are all lovingly described within these pages. You'll also learn about the less glamorous side of sewage: the world of cesspits, septic tanks, and treatment plants – smelly, but vital, facilities that are so often belittled or ignored.

As well as the historical and technical aspects of the toilet, *Now Wash Your Hands* looks at the human side of the commode: the language, the customs and superstitions, and the – often revolting – behaviour that has become associated with this very necessary invention. And, as if all this weren't enough, the text also takes a fascinating trip down the slimy roller-coaster that is the human intestinal tract, musing on the substance we are so anxious to get rid of – crap. What is it? Where does it come from? Where is it going? If you don't know now, you soon will do.

A number of people helped me in my research for this book and I'd like to offer them my thanks. They are: Andrew Goodfellow, Julie Adams, Mike Haskins, Jan West, Caroline F. McDonald, Eugene Griessel, Mia Sharona, Gord Beaman, Jerry Miller, Will Ryan, John R. Nickolls, John Hairell, Malcolm Duncan, Richard Woodward, and Kirk Stant.

HISTORY OF THE TOILET

PART ONE

Ancient Loos

Having a crap was never a problem for our nomadic ancestors – when the area around a campsite became too filthy the whole tribe upped sticks and moved somewhere else. The tribesmen of Siberia regarded cities as cursed (and perhaps still do) because their inhabitants had to live among their own dung. Disposing of sewage was a problem for these early city dwellers, and only the very rich could afford anything approaching modern convenience. Yet evidence everywhere suggests that wherever nomadic man put down roots, he put down loos soon after.

In the third millennium BC, in Mesopotamia, King Sargon had a palace equipped with six privies. These were holes with U-shaped seats that drained into a sophisticated sewer system. Most houses weren't connected to sewers and relied on cesspits. Poorer inhabitants probably threw their excrement into the street. As a half-hearted hygiene measure these crap and garbage-strewn roads were periodically resurfaced with a layer of clay and houses gradually had to be rebuilt to keep up with the rising street level.

In India there seems to have been sophisticated plumbing arrangements in the Indus valley as early as 2500 BC. Archaeologists studying the Harappa ruins at Lothal have discovered houses connected to a sewer system that boasted manholes and inspection chambers. These privies were built as an attachment to a bathing room and were equipped with brick or wooden seats. Sadly, the decline of the Indus civilisation soon resulted in a rapid return to alfresco crapping for most people. In later years the Mughal kings were quite fond of their conveniences, or *gushalkhana*, and built many luxurious bathrooms and toilets.

The toilet also has a long history in China, a recent find being the bathroom of a Western Han Dynasty king in Henan. Built roughly 2000 years ago the toilet is a sit-down flushing affair equipped with comfortable armrests. The toilet is part of a tomb complex built so that the deceased royal could enjoy all the comforts of home in the afterlife.

On the island of Crete the Minoan palace of Knossus had spectacular plumbing. Built in around 1800 BC the royal washrooms were equipped with bathtubs and wooden seated toilets supplied with piped water. Such facilities would only have been used by a lucky few, however. On the mainland the early Greeks were not shy about defecation and used the great outdoors as a privy. Although most Greeks seem to have been happy crouching behind a bush it seems there were a few who preferred privacy; in one of the plays of Aristophanes an old priest complains that people only visit his temple to crap in it. In later centuries the houses of rich Greeks had flushing privies connected to underground sewers, while commoners made use of chamber pots and communal cesspits.

The outdoor ablutions of the early Greeks contrasted dramatically with those of the Egyptians. The latter believed that unsavoury, but necessary, acts should be carried out in private, and they relieved themselves indoors. The Greek historian Herodotus remarked that the Egyptians defecated indoors and ate out of doors, whereas the Greeks did it the other way round. Archaeologists have dated the earliest Egyptian sit-down toilets as far back as 2100 BC. Egyptian loos had limestone seats equipped with keyhole-shaped openings that were positioned over a removable pot, or a dish of sand. As with the Chinese tombs mentioned above, the royal graves of the second dynasty were often equipped with lavatory chambers for the benefit of the dead Pharaoh.

The Romans

Roman toilets were very advanced. Most Romans relieved themselves in public latrines, or *foricae*, of which Rome boasted 144 by AD315. They were communal affairs in which the patrons sat side by side on a wooden bench full of holes. Directly beneath the holes a trough of running water drained into a sewer or cesspit. Some of these toilets sat 40 people at a time. A communal sponge on a stick was provided for bottom-wiping purposes. This was kept in a jar of salt water and after use it was replaced for the next patron (*see* Wiping Up, p. 00). It would appear that Roman toilets were not divided between the sexes, but since most people wore long togas there was little chance of anyone exposing themselves unduly.

Richer private homes had their own lavatories usually consisting of a hole in the floor positioned over a cesspit. They were usually located near the kitchen so that they could also be used for the disposal of kitchen scraps. A few houses were connected to a piped water supply and had flushing lavatories that drained into a sewer.

The main sewer of Rome was the Cloaca Maxima built between 800 BC and 735 BC. The sewage system was designed principally to drain rainwater and replaced an earlier system of open trenches leading to the Tiber. In time the sewers came to be used to dispose of everything from household waste to dead criminals and had to be kept clear by gangs of slaves. Connection to a sewer was an expensive business for which a licence was required, which meant that only the most wealthy could afford it.

Despite the lavish provision of public toilets many Romans still found themselves caught short on occasion, often resorting to the privacy of the nearest temple or holy grove to relieve themselves. To put a stop to this sacrilege the authorities put up signs warning that the gods were watching and would not be pleased by this grubby behaviour. Even graveyards and tombs weren't safe. Some Roman gravestones had warnings inscribed on them such as, 'Whoever pisses or shits here will provoke the gods above and below'. Loo graffiti was also a concern; to stop people writing on toilet walls they were decorated with portraits of the gods to make people think twice about desecrating sacred images. It didn't always work; in the ruins of Herculaneum, near Pompeii, the message 'APOLLONIVS MEDICVS TITI IMP HIC CACARIT BENE' was found written on a toilet wall. Translated it reads, 'Apollonius, physician of Emperor Titus, had a good crap here'. What a charmer.

Medieval Loos

In medieval Europe castle toilets were known as 'garderobes' and some doubled as wardrobes. During the summer months heavy winter cloaks and furs would be stored in the privy in the belief that the draught from the toilet shaft kept moths at bay (the smell probably helped too). These privies were often built in a chamber or buttress that protruded from the outer wall of a castle giving excrement a clear vertical drop to the ground. As a primitive heating measure many garderobes were built near chimney flues leading from the kitchen. Larger communal loos would be built in an inside room that was equipped with a diagonal waste shaft leading to an outer wall, the shaft sometimes emerging from the mouth of a grimacing gargoyle. To help keep them clean many of these channels were designed so that rainwater funnelled through them.

An unfortunate by-product of a garderobe was a huge skid mark running down the wall beneath it. To conceal this unpleasant brown staining more fastidious castle owners built hollow flues to act as discreet vertical poop-chutes.

Some garderobes were the Achilles' heel of a castle's defences. If they were large enough, it was possible for enemy troops to climb up them (though volunteers would presumably have been hard to come by). In France, in 1204, the Château Gaillard was stormed in this way.

Occasionally a modern traveller will come across a garderobe in working order. In Russia's Lake Lodoga there's a garderobe-like toilet in an old monastery on the island of Valaam. Visitors can use the primitive toilet facilities but a constant updraft means that any toilet paper thrown down the poop-chute will fly straight back in your face.

At Hampton Court there was a spectacular communal privy known as the House of Easement. Used by the courtiers of Henry VIII it was on two floors and could seat up to 28 people at a time. As in Roman communal toilets the patrons sat on a long plank with holes in it, the waste dropping down a chute into a culvert from where it travelled to the River Thames via the moat. King Henry didn't sit with the riff-raff, however; he had his own commode. Henry's drains were kept clean by a professional 'scourer' named Philip Long who employed a small band of, probably rather stinky, children armed with rakes and scrapers to help do the job.

Abbeys and monasteries were often equipped with loos, sometimes known as 'reredorters'. These were usually built on the Roman model consisting of wooden seating over a gutter of running water. As in the Hampton Court privy, these abbey loos were large communal affairs. The life of the monks was very ordered and they frequently had to go to the toilet together at set times. Unlike the Roman loos, the monastery stalls were separated by partitions to protect the monks' privacy. The Abbot of St Albans (consecrated in AD1115) had a private loo flushed by a rainwater cistern – the first recorded flushing toilet in England.

Many European cities had communal public privies. In some cases they might have been as efficient and clean as the monastery toilets but most consisted of primitive seating arrangements over an open cesspit. Most people went in the open, or used a chamber pot at home and threw the contents into the street.

Getting rid of excrement was a problem. In 1321 a London woman illegally connected her privy to a rain gutter and was fined when she eventually blocked it. In the same year, London's Ebbegate Lane became blocked by effluent falling from second-storey privies, and in 1347 two men were arrested for connecting their privy to their neighbour's cellar. A special body called the 'scavenger court' was created to resolve these waste disputes, one notable case being that of John Davis who complained that the inhabitants of an entire London street were dumping their dung on his property.

Most waste ended up in the river. The houses on London Bridge were served by a public toilet jutting over the Thames, and the Fleet River collected the effluent of 11 public privies and three sewers. Not surprisingly, some nearby monks complained that the stink of the Fleet had, 'overcome the frankincense burnt at the altar', and claimed that the fumes had caused the deaths of several brothers.

The Sewage Professionals

The people responsible for cleaning and emptying cesspits were known variously as 'scourers', 'gongfermors', 'rakers', 'night-soil men', or just 'nightmen'. Their job was a nasty but relatively well-paid one. In 1281, 13 men were paid triple-time over five days to clean the cesspit of Newgate prison.

Many people avoided paying for the services of the nightmen by throwing their sewage into the gutter. These drains and ditches soon became clogged with excrement and regularly overflowed into the streets. In medieval Paris entrepreneurs known as *pontonniers volants* ('flying pontoon makers') bridged these flooded sewers with a plank and charged people to walk across them. Medieval Paris seems to have had a particularly bad sewage problem. At one time 2300 night-soil carts were needed to empty the privies of the Paris tenement blocks. The city defences even had to be rebuilt when it became clear that the human dunghill outside the city walls had grown so large it could be used by attackers as an 'offensive' platform.

Loo Laws

Various countries tried to legislate against dung dumping. In 14th century England, Richard II passed a law stating that 'none shall cast any garbage or dung or filth into ditches', and a programme of public privy-building was launched to encourage people to defecate in sanctioned areas. In France, legislation was passed in 1514 requiring every home in Paris to have a privy, and in 1519 the government ordered that all French households should have a cesspit. Back in England, Henry VIII passed an edict requiring all householders to clean any sewer passing by their dwelling, and he set up a Commission of Sewers to enforce the new regulations. Unfortunately Henry did not budget adequately for the Commission and it wasn't until 1622 that it was finally installed.

Among those who fell foul of the new laws was

Shakespeare's father, who was fined for not keeping his gutter clean. Even the clergy were not above the law; the rector of St Botolph's was called before the Assize of Nuisances for allowing piles of dung to accumulate around his new privy.

Threepenny Bits

IN 4th century Rome a tax (the Chrysargyron) was levied on all excrement and urine.

THE Domesday Book records that there was a fine for anyone found crapping inside Chester Cathedral.

THE herring fishermen on the Isle of Skye used to have a toilet known in Gaelic as the *Rendha an fhaileadh*, the 'place of smells'.

THE first written reference to crapping was in 700 BC. The Assyrian emperor, Sennacherib, appeared on the battlefield causing his enemies, the kings of Babylon and Elam, to 'let their dung go in their chariots'.

ARCHAEOLOGISTS have discovered a cave dweller's toilet in Nevada. It's seven centimetres deep in fossilised poo.

IN medieval Paris people often shared elevated privies built between the second floors of neighbouring houses. People frequently fell through the rotting floorboards onto the dunghill below.

PATENT WASH-DOWN TRITON CLOSET.

MADE IN FINEST IVORY OR WHITEWARE PORCELAIN.

This ideal Closet possesses the advantages of the Valve Closet without its disadvantages.

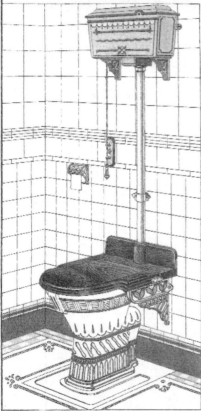

No. 145.—Triton Closet Suite.

Attention is called to the unique form of the Improved Triton Closet, affording such great water area, and yet capable of being successfully cleansed by a 3 gallons flush. The Patent Drip Soleplate has been designed to enable the plumber to make a reliable gas-tight joint, especially with the S Trap Closet. This system, which overcomes well-known objections, is of high sanitary value, and has met with considerable approval.

No. 142.—Triton Closet.

Patent Fire-clay Drip Sole.

No. 145.—Patent Triton Closet Suite comprises—

		£	s.
No.	3, Enamel Painted 3 gallons Cistern ...	1	10
„	198, Cistern Brackets, Decorated... ...	0	2
„	147, Bracket Pull and Chain	0	4
„	198, Polished Copper Pipe... ...	0	16
„	146, Walnut Seat	1	12
„	141, Seat Brackets, Decorated	0	8
„	142A, Ivoryware Closet, Decorated and best gilt	4	7
„	143, Patent Drip Sole, fitted	0	17
„	210, Paper Case, Embossed Brass ...	0	10
	Price of Suite as shewn... ...	£10	10

No. 142.—Triton Closet in Finest Ivoryware, S or P Trap, and with or without Vent ... 40/-

„ 142B.—Do. do. Decorated in colors ... 53/6

„ 142A.—Do. do. do. and picked out in best gold ... 87/6

„ 146A.—If with Polished Copper Buffer Plate fitted under front of seat to prevent urine trickling down front of Closet... 2/4 extra

HISTORY OF THE TOILET

PART TWO

Into the Modern Age

Sanitary arrangements had changed little in centuries by the time of the Renaissance. The wealthy had their own privies; the poor used chamber pots, public conveniences, or went in the gutter. People seemed to be quite indiscriminate in their toilet habits, to the extent that Leonardo da Vinci proposed building homes with spiral staircases to stop the residents from crapping on the landings.

People, it seems, would go anywhere. The artist Hogarth was once caught short in a churchyard and dropped his trousers over a grave. His appalled friend discouraged him by beating his bare bottom with some nettles whereupon Hogarth moved to a more respectful location – by the church doors! Even palaces were not safe. In France, Henry IV had to ban pissing in the corridors of the Louvre Palace, and in 1764 an English visitor to Versailles described it as 'the receptacle of all the horrors of mankind' the reason being that, 'the passageways, the courtyards ... the corridors are filled with urine and faeces'.

The French nobility seem to have been rather lax in their toilet habits. Anne of Austria (mother of King Louis XIV) was once caught pissing behind a tapestry, and in 1606 the *Dauphin* (the Crown Prince) was found peeing against the wall of his bedchamber in St Germain Palace. Some British nobles weren't much better: in 1666 an Oxford resident complained that the entourage of the visiting Charles II had left excrement in every corner, chimney, and coal house.

With the passage of time, efforts were made to regulate domestic sanitary arrangements. As far as the authorities were concerned the ideal situation was for each house to have its own cesspit which could be periodically cleaned and its contents carted away for disposal. Many people still clung to the old ways however. In 1760, the citizens of Madrid almost revolted when the king threatened to impose the use of sewers and privies. Some people thought excrement in the streets was positively healthy as it was believed that dung drew impurities out of the air. After the imposition of sewers, some Spaniards built their privy in the kitchen so that their excrement would cleanse the atmosphere and make their food more wholesome.

By the 18th century most city households in England had a cesspit, though some people weren't too fussy about emptying it. Samuel Pepys recorded in 1660 that 'going down to my cellar … I put my feet into a great heap of turds, by which I find that Mrs Turner's house of office is full and comes into my cellar'. As can be gathered from this incident the cesspit system was far from perfect but it did mean that most waste was disposed of properly and didn't find its way into the nearest river or well. However, this situation was to change dramatically with the popularisation of the water closet in the early 19th century.

The Water Closet

As more and more people installed WCs (i.e. flushing toilets), the amount of water used by households grew enormously. In London, for example, water use more than doubled between 1850 and 1856. Household cesspits could not cope with the amount of fluid generated by flushing loos and they soon started to overflow, often contaminating sources of drinking water. In London the problem was solved by connecting household cesspits to sewers and channelling effluent to the Thames. Previously these sewers had only been used for the drainage of rainwater, and whereas before 1815 it had been illegal to discharge sewage into a sewer, after 1847 it became illegal not to. Not surprisingly the Thames soon became overwhelmed and after 'the Great Stink' of 1858 (which forced the abandonment of the Houses of Parliament) a new drainage scheme was installed that intercepted the old sewers and removed the waste far downstream.

The First Modern Loo

The invention of the modern water closet is attributed to Sir John Harington (godson to Queen Elizabeth) in 1596. Sir John, a noted wit, scholar and ladies' man, was known for his fastidious habits (he bathed daily), although it's not altogether clear why he was inspired to design a flush lavatory. The slang for a privy at this time was the 'jakes', and Harington punningly named his invention the 'Ajax'. Detailed designs for the Ajax together with estimated building costs (6s and 8d) were recorded in a pamphlet that included bad puns, off-colour stories, and satirical digs at prominent figures. Initially the Queen was not impressed by Harington's work and had him banished from Court for his bad taste. However she later relented and had an Ajax installed at Richmond Palace. Unfortunately most people regarded Sir John as a laughing stock and, apart from a second Ajax installed in his own home, he never built another.

Toilet Types

After the Ajax, water closets of various sorts were built over the centuries but little is known of them. These contraptions would have been built to order by craftsmen for those rich enough to afford a supply of piped water. There are few records of what these pioneers looked like or how they operated, but most early WCs were probably 'plug closets'.

The Ajax was a simple plug closet – essentially a bowl with a hole in the bottom stopped with a plug on the end of a stick. To empty the bowl you would pull on the stick to lift the plug, then flush out the bowl's contents. Not surprisingly the stick, plug and the hole soon became encrusted with filth. Some might have been equipped with an in-built water-trap to stop smells rising from the sewer.

Next on the evolutionary toilet ladder were 'pan closets' – bottomless basins that funnelled waste into a water-filled copper pan. The lower rim of the basin was below the water level in the pan so the water formed a 'seal' that kept out sewer smells. After use a lever was pulled to drop the contents of the pan into the sewer pipe or cesspit. The bowl and pan were then washed with a flush of water from a cistern.

In 1775, Alexander Cumming, a Scottish watchmaker,

became the first person to patent a water closet. His version consisted of a metal basin containing a few inches of water, and a sliding valve at the bottom. After use a lever was pulled to slide the valve open and let the water and excrement drop down. The same action released a flush of water from a cistern. Cumming's design incorporated an S-bend in the outflow pipe (though he didn't invent it) and this helped to keep the stink at bay. A cabinet-maker named Joseph Bramah refined Cumming's design in 1778 by adding a hinge to the valve system which cut down on leakage and improved efficiency. Bramah's design was mass-produced and 6,000 of them had been sold by 1797.

The main disadvantage of these early closets was that they were mechanically complicated and impossible to keep clean without dismantling them. Having said that, filthy pan closets were still being made up to 1891 and many antique lavatories survived well into the 20th century. Indeed, a working Bramah can still found in the House of Lords in the 'Prince Consort's Room', currently occupied by Lord Hailsham.

Wash-out Closets

The next WC revolution came around 1870 with the invention of the 'wash-out closet'. This dropped the unsanitary valve and relied on the S-bend to act as a seal. A reservoir of water was held in the bowl by a lip, and after use the water and excrement was flushed over the lip, past the S-bend, through the soil pipe, and into the sewers. The flush had to be powerful to work properly and many manufacturers built their WCs with elevated cisterns to increase the force of the water.

One of the main wash-out manufacturers was Thomas Twyford. Cheap to manufacture, his simple earthenware WCs were easy to keep clean and less likely to go wrong. Modified wash-out closets are still made today and are popular on the Continent (*see* Crappers of All Nations, p. 159).

Wash-down Closets

This is essentially the toilet used today in Britain and the USA. In the 'wash-down', excrement falls into a pool of water held by the S-bend. There is no 'lip' to get past and the force of the flush is used more effectively. Put simply, a turd in a wash-out closet has three corners to get round, whereas there are only two in a wash-down.

There is evidence to suggest that the London firm of Humphersons were responsible for inventing this design; they started building their one-piece wash-down model 'the Beufort' in around 1885.

The Siphonic Flush

Another important Victorian invention was the 'water waste preventer' or 'siphonic flush'. Some say that the legendary, and unfortunately named, Thomas Crapper invented this but it seems to have been the work of Joseph Adamson. He patented the first siphonic flush in 1853. This eliminated leaks from cisterns which had become a source of alarm to the water companies because of the water wastage that resulted.

Some toilets use a 'double-trap siphonic action', first patented in 1870 by John Mann. Here, the water in the bowl suffers a 'double whammy': it is sucked down out of the bowl by air pressure and simultaneously flushed down by the rush of water. In Britain double-trap toilets were popular until well into the 20th century but have now largely been ousted by cheaper models.

Other Types of WC

In the 18th and 19th centuries the cheapest flushing toilet available was the 'hopper' which looked like an upturned flower pot or dunce's cap. It's not known who first started manufacturing hopper closets but they might have predated the plug and pan closets and were still being made in Britain in 1910. Some hoppers were glazed, decorated, and equipped with a wooden seating surround, however more often than not you had to sit on the bare rim. Because of their cheapness they were often bought for use in factories, schools and prisons.

The 'trough' was also designed for use in factories and prisons. It resembled a cattle feeder (hence its name), with a trickle of water running down its length. There were two models, a 12-footer and a 24-footer, the latter designed to seat up to eight people at a time.

The 'tipper-closet' was a flush WC designed for people without a regular water supply. It consisted of a trough balanced on a pivot. Waste water would be emptied into the trough via a slop hole or sink and when the trough was full it would topple over under its own weight and dump the water down the privy. The trough would then right itself ready to be filled again. This was a good way to conserve water in areas where there was no piped water, or only an intermittent supply. Some cisterns used a small internal tipper to flush automatically when they were full.

Threepenny Bits

JAMES I of England enjoyed hunting so much that he wouldn't leave the saddle even to go the toilet. He'd go in his pants and have his servants wipe him off when he got home.

IN England the first lay house to have underground drainage was Westminster Palace. The drains were installed in the reign of Henry III; formerly there had only been an open sewer.

IN Regency England the outside privies of the wealthy were sometimes disguised as Grecian temples.

THE British Army Regiment the '14th/20th King's Hussars' are known as the 'Emperor's Chambermaids' as, during the Battle of Vittoria in 1813, they captured the silver chamber pot of the king of Spain, Joseph Bonaparte. The pot is now used as a giant goblet.

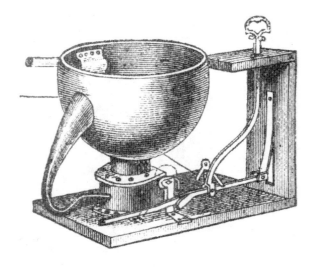

'Blue Magnolia Design', 1895

'Raised Acanthus Pattern', 1895

'Pedestal Lion' Closet

'The Lambeth', 1895

'Mulberry Peach Decoration', 1890

HISTORY OF THE TOILET

PART THREE

The Golden Age of the WC

In the 18th century flushing water closets were novelties that were distinctly unpopular in some quarters. In 1770 Mr Melmouth of Bath installed a WC (probably a pan closet) and promptly had his water supply cut off amid complaints from the water company that his new lavatory would use an inordinate amount of water. They refused to reconnect him until it was removed.

Water closets slowly gained ground over the years, a significant number having been installed in London households by the 1830s. However they really took off with the Great Exhibition of 1851. Not only were a number of models on display but the public toilets at the exhibition gave many people an opportunity to 'test drive' a WC.

Brand Preference

THE toilet business was fiercely competitive and dozens if not hundreds of competing models were produced. Some of the most prominent manufacturers of the Victorian era were Humphersons, Shanks, Ducketts, Armitage, Jennings, Crapper, Doultons, Hellyers and Twyford and the enormous range of models they produced included the: Alaska, Alerto, Aqua Jet, Aquarius, Arthurlie, Aztec, Beaufort, Cascade, Champion, Citizen, Clencher, Closet of the Century, Comet, County Council, Deluge, Desideratum, Directo, Dolphin, Dreadnought, Empire, Eureka, Excelsior, Frigidas, Granitas, Hebas, Hindoostan, Indoro, Junction, Lambeth Patent Pedestal, Latestas, Liernas, Lion, Metropole, National, Native Bombay, New Humber, Niagra, Optimus, Oracle, Oriental, Orion, Ormonde, Paisley, Pefecta, Perfectus, Perfect Elastic Valve Closet, Precipitas, Rapid, Rapide, Rapidus, Ribble, Ripple, Rivoline, Rocket, Royal, Ryastas, Sanitas, Seestu, Shakespeare, Shower, Siberia, Solidus, Square Embossed Primo, Storm, Sultan, Swift, Tobasco, Trent, Unitas, United Corbel, Unus, Vistula, Watervaal, and the Zeta.

The Golden Age of Toilet began in the 1870s with the introduction of the all-ceramic wash-down and wash-out closets. The earlier valve and pan closets had complex mechanisms that needed to be concealed by a wooden surround, but the new ceramic 'pedestal' closets were entirely visible and, as a consequence, became highly decorated. Some were built in the shape of lions, some as dolphins and elephants, others were decorated with raised ornamentation incorporating flowers, fruits, shells, and ornate scrolls. Many were covered in elaborate and colourful underglaze patterns: some had Grecian friezes, others the Willow Pattern or pictures of Windsor Castle, and some were even gilded. The ornamentation became so lavish that toilets started to rival china tableware in opulence. Some said they resembled giant soup bowls.

British WC manufacturers became renowned for the quality of their wares and sold WCs all over the world. The Russians were so impressed by this craftsmanship that they adopted 'Unitas' (the name of an early all-ceramic closet made by Twyford) as an alternative word for 'excellence'.

Selling WCs

Perhaps the best marketing ploy for a new WC was to obtain royal approval. One of the reasons why Thomas Crapper achieved such prominence is that he was asked to overhaul the royal toilet facilities at Sandringham. As a result he was allowed to display the royal coat of arms on his wares. There are also manholes inside Westminster Abbey that still bear the name T. Crapper. However, contrary to popular belief, he was never knighted for his services.

The Edward Johns company (now part of Armitage Shanks) once got into trouble for displaying 'By Appointment' on their WCs without permission. Asked to remove the royal arms the company declined and used the words, 'Not by Appointment' instead.

Manufacturers also became very inventive when it came to WC gadgetry. An early problem with WCs was that the uninitiated didn't realise that the wooden seat had to be put down before use. To encourage people to do this some toilet rims came equipped with ceramic spikes. Automatic flushing toilets were also very popular: Doulton's 'seat-action closets' came in two varieties – those that flushed when you got up (an idea first patented in 1792), and those that flushed continuously when you were seated. To keep seats free from urine splashes some seats automatically raised themselves when they weren't being sat on. Unfortunately some seats were known to rise too quickly giving the departing patron a smack on the backside.

Flush Testing

Apart from a WC's appearance and the quality of its craftsmanship, the strength of its flush was also a major selling point. At trade fairs and exhibitions rival WC makers would demonstrate the flushing power of their latest creations by disposing of a variety of objects. At an exhibition of 1884 George Jenning's 'pedestal vase' managed to dispose of ten apples, one flat sponge, three 'air vessels', a quantity of plumber's smudge and four pieces of paper stuck to the inside of the bowl. (The air vessels were artificial 'floaters' made out of twists of paper and looking rather like Christmas crackers.) Other manufacturers had their own flushing favourites: Thomas Crapper liked flushing cotton waste and grease, and one WC maker (some say Crapper) once flushed his assistant's cloth cap. More recently, even ping-pong balls have been disposed of by super-flushing toilets.

WC manufacturers still test their products in this way today. One Japanese firm has developed artificial faeces, a clay-like mass which is measured out into 400g lumps and rolled into shape by hand. These 'pseudo turds' are then garnished with wads of toilet paper and flushed. There are also national standard tests that all manufacturers must perform. In America these include flushing away a number of small plastic balls, disposing of a 'sludge' made of plastic granules, and removing ink stains on the inside of the bowl. The US Consumer Union performs its own tests using home-made turds. These are created out of sawdust and flour with some hollow plastic beads mixed in to provide buoyancy.

The Toilet in America

The history of American toilets is very similar to those in Britain although the problems of urban congestion did not strike until much later.

In most US cities houses were equipped with cesspits but there were the usual problems with people dumping their refuse into the street – a practice that was frequently legislated against. As in Europe, waste from the cesspits was dug, or pumped, out and taken away in carts. In New York's early days it was usual to throw this waste in the sea and there are stories of small boats being sunk by a sudden deluge of effluent. As the city expanded and the waters grew more polluted it was decided to dump waste in neighbouring New Jersey. However this was a short-term measure and in the 1870s it was decided to install a proper city-wide sewage system.

Little House on the Prairie

As in Europe most American homes had an 'outhouse', usually strategically placed between 50 and 150 feet away from the main dwelling. If possible they were also situated downhill from the nearest well to prevent contamination, although such precautions did not always work.

In the 18th century a Dr Benjamin Rush discovered an unpleasant-tasting well in his back garden. Health spas were all the rage at the time and the local townsfolk decided that anything tasting so distinctive must be full of health-giving properties. They drank the well dry only to discover it was connected to the doctor's cesspit.

Some outhouses were dangerous in other ways. In the 18th century the owner of the Michie Tavern in Virginia installed a safety rope in his privy pit so that anyone falling in could pull themselves out. Apparently this was a common problem and he was tired of being called out to rescue floundering guests.

The traditional outhouse was a wooden shack containing a seat over a pit four or five feet deep. Most seats were one-holers but many had two or more. Lye was sometimes sprinkled down the hole to kill maggots but apart from that the sewage was left to its own devices. When the pit was full it could be shovelled out by hand or, more usually, a new pit would be dug and the outhouse shack moved over it. In some parts of the country it was traditional to plant a fruit tree sapling over an old privy pit. The young tree acted as a marker and benefited from the storehouse of nutrients under its roots.

Outhouses were traditionally built with a crescent moon or star-shaped hole in the door. These holes provided some light and ventilation and it's been suggested that they also acted as 'his' and 'hers' signs – moons for the ladies, stars for the gentlemen. Most outhouses seem to have been unisex however.

An American innovation that developed alongside the outhouse was the 'slop-jar' – a bucket with a lid used for carrying the contents of chamber pots. Since the outhouses of America were usually quite a distance from the main dwelling the 'spill-proof' slop-jar was probably more secure than an open-topped pot.

Threepenny Bits

In Victorian England toilet seats were sometimes referred to as 'haunch pieces'.

In some 19th-century American cities, slums, schools and prisons were equipped with large communal lavatories. They were called 'sink schools' as 'schools' of people used them.

The First Lord of Grimthorpe, the designer of Big Ben, built a loo that locked you in until you'd flushed the bowl.

The 'Swamp Angels' were a gang of 19th-century New York criminals who used the city sewers as their base.

In the 19th century the king of Portugal toured the new sewers of Paris in a boat.

Outhouses are still found in many parts of America. It's been estimated that 200,000 households in North Carolina have an outhouse, or pipe waste directly into a river (an illegal practice). Poor sanitation is a country-wide problem, and the 1990 census revealed that in Virginia there are 46,000 homes without proper plumbing (and 28,000 in Florida, 27,500 in Alabama, 22,000 in Mississippi, 32,000 in Tennessee, 69,000 in California, and 67,000 in New York).

WC USA

According to legend the first WC installed in America belonged to the poet and Harvard professor Henry Wadsworth Longfellow (1807-82), however it was not until the 1870s that they were imported in large numbers. At the time British lavatories were the best in the world and manufacturers in the USA had a hard time selling their wares. One of these was Thomas Maddock, a former pottery decorator from Staffordshire. Maddock struggled to make American WCs that would compete with the British imports but American buyers were wary of domestic products. To encourage sales Maddock stamped his bowls with a lion and a unicorn and the words 'Best Stafford Earthenware made for the American Market'.

How Long is Plumbing "Up to Date"

GOOD plumbing should have more than a utility value. It should be in keeping with your ideas of refinement. It should harmonize with your other modern home furnishings and equipment.

Fixtures meaning so much in appearance and service naturally are being improved constantly. Styles and designs of years ago may still have a service value, but are being replaced with the more attractive and sanitary fixtures now in vogue.

Is Your Plumbing Ten Years Old?

If so, it is time to remodel; to install new up-to-date fixtures in Bath, Kitchen and Laundry. Why wait until plumbing fixtures become noticeably obsolete or fail to function properly before being replaced? There is hardly any other equipment in your home tried so frequently. Your home life is what you make

it. Years roll by quickly. Why wait and put off improvements which mean so much day by day? Possibly your home should have more bathrooms, one for at least each two bedrooms.

Picture your bathroom with a "Standard" Built-in Bath. A big smart-lip tub, built right into the floor and walls. No open spaces left below and behind the tub, so difficult to keep clean. Unquestionably a more sanitary fixture.

Send for Your Plumber

Do not wait until your present fixtures get out of order. If your plumbing has not been inspected lately it may need attention right now. Weakened joints caused by settling of the building may have developed unseen leaks. Rubber washers deteriorate in time—waste pipes and traps collect sediment and should be inspected from time to time.

Write us for a copy of "Standard" Plumbing Fixtures for the Home." It describes modern and beautiful fixtures for bathrooms, kitchen and laundry.

Standard Sanitary Mfg. Co., Pittsburgh, Pa.

HISTORY OF THE TOILET

PART FOUR

Today's Toilets and Beyond

Sadly, the gorgeous creations of the Victorian WC manufacturers lost their colours and opulent decorations in the early 20th century. Sleek lines and a plain finish became the fashion and have remained so ever since. There are a few companies that still manufacture retro-designs but they are generally quite expensive. One example is the Nautilus II, a lion-shaped toilet based on a popular Victorian design. Because they are so highly decorated, and the casting procedure so complex (only 16 per cent of the toilets survive the process), each Nautilus costs in excess of £2000. Another is the Dolphin Suite made by Armitage Shanks, a model that was originally manufactured by the company in the 1870s. The dolphin is curled into an 'S' shape and holds a fluted shell (the bowl) in its mouth.

Low-flush Toilets

Whereas the WC manufactures of yesteryear treated water as an unlimited resource, the emphasis today is on water conservation. In many parts of the world conservation measures mean that toilets that would once have used 3-5 gallons of water per flush may now only use 1.6 gallons. This has caused all sorts of problems with 'incomplete flushing' forcing many people to invest in a plunger. In fact, some of the less well-designed low-flush toilets can end up using more water than the old ones as people have to clean the bowl with two or three small flushes rather than one big one. There's also a problem in that many modern low-flush toilets don't work well when hooked up with old plumbing systems.

Some Modern Toilet Types

POWER-FLUSH TOILETS – A particular problem in old houses are cast-iron pipes with rough inner surfaces. The old 'high-flush' toilets could force waste through these flow-resistant pipes but feeble low-flush lavatories need a hand. One solution is a pressurised cistern that uses compressed air to force waste down the pipe. Mains pressure is used to compress the air in a sealed cistern. When the toilet is flushed the compressed air forces out the water like a jet.

VACUUM-POWERED TOILETS – Here the cistern consists of two internal water tanks. The tanks are arranged so that flushing creates an internal vacuum that forces water into the bowl. There's only a rim flush so theoretically this design will keep the bowl cleaner than other models.

DUAL FLUSH TOILETS – Some low-flush loos are equipped with two handles. One of these delivers a full 1.6 gallon flush, the other a smaller 1.1 gallon flush. You decide what's needed depending on what you've left in the bowl.

SINK TOILETS – These channel the used 'grey' water from an adjoining handbasin unit into the cistern of a toilet. This way no fresh water is used for flushing.

High-tech Toilets

Japan leads the market in high-tech toilets, one company in particular, Toto, being famous for its luxurious loos. High-tech loos can come with a combination of any of the following features:

ELEVATING SEATS – A mechanised toilet seat tilts up and down, designed to help the elderly and infirm get on and off.

SELF-RAISING LIDS – These sense your presence and lift the toilet lid when you enter the bathroom. When you leave, the lid goes down.

SEAT WARMERS – These are especially appreciated in Japan where many houses are not centrally heated.

SEAT COVERS/CLEANERS – In America, paper 'toilet seat shields' are sometimes known as 'butt-gaskets'. Usually these are placed on by hand but in some cases the toilet seat revolves after use and the paper cover is replaced automatically. A variation on this design is a damp brush that cleans the seat as it revolves. Some toilets are made with an 'anti-bacterial' glaze that will (hopefully) kill germs before they get a foothold.

WARM-WATER BIDETS – These remove the need for toilet paper and some water sprays can be set to 'pulse' to give your botty a massage. Unfortunately these bidets do sometimes cause problems. High-tech loos with many features often have complex control panels and it's not unknown for the uninitiated to press the 'bidet button' rather than the 'flush button'. More often than not this will result in soaked clothes and a wet bathroom floor. Bidet loos are particularly popular in Japan. This might have something to do with the fact that piles – a condition often irritated by the use of toilet paper – are common in Japan with one-third of the population said to be sufferers.

DRYERS – For use in conjunction with a bidet, these toilets dry off your bottom with a waft of warm air.

AIR FILTERS – Air from the toilet bowl is drawn down through a series of deodorising filters to help reduce noxious smells.

SPEAKERS – These play Muzak or make the sound of running water to mask any unpleasant noises the user might be generating.

UV LAMPS – These help to kill off any germs lurking on loo surfaces.

UPGRADING – One American company manufactures a loo 'upgrade-kit' that enables you to jazz up your old-fashioned toilet. They make a product called IntiMist which is basically a high-tech toilet seat that can be fitted to your old loo. The IntiMist features a seat-warmer and two warm-water bidet sprays.

Medi-Loos

Another type of high-tech Japanese loo will analyse your urine, take your blood pressure, record your weight and work out your proportion of body fat. All this information can then be sent direct to your doctor via an in-built modem. In Germany, special 'radiation loos' have been built for the use of nuclear workers. They measure the level of radiation in the workers' urine and alert them to any problems.

Incinerator Toilets

These are usually found in areas where it is impossible to connect a toilet to a sewer. They use electricity to reduce excrement to an ash that can be thrown out with the trash. There are plans afoot to design a 'microwave' toilet that will do the same.

Macerating Toilets

These chew up your turds in the same way a waste-disposal unit mashes kitchen scraps. In some cases it is impossible to install a toilet with a normal outflow pipe. Grinding up waste means it can be forced through a much smaller tube.

The Peacekeeper

This American toilet has no flush handle. The toilet only flushes when you put down the seat. This means there are no more arguments about the seat being up or down, hence the name. A similar Canadian invention is called the Considerate Seat, a gravity-powered seat that gently closes itself two minutes after being raised.

Glow-in-the-dark Seats

These are a great boon to those visiting the loo in the night. However you can also upgrade your existing seat by the application of special photoluminescent stickers round the inside of the rim.

GOING TO THE LOO

Squatting versus Sitting

Eastern tradition dictates squatting to defecate, while in the West it's more usual to sit (*see* Crappers of All Nations, p.159). Squatting is said to be the healthier option as it aligns the rectum and anus in a near-vertical position. Sitting tends to create a kink between the rectum and anus often necessitating much straining to force a turd around the bend. Squatting also spreads the buttocks to reveal the anus, whereas sitting can do the opposite.

Unfortunately squatting does require considerable leg strength and can be very tricky if you're not used to it. A number of Western tourists have put their backs out or locked their knees trying to use a squat toilet on holiday. Rising after a squat can also be a problem for the elderly and many squat loos are equipped with supports to help the old folks clamber upright.

Dress code also plays an important role in the squat/sit divide. Squatting is fine if you're wearing an Arab robe or Japanese kimono, but for those dressed in trousers it's more problematic. Squatting with trousers round your ankles is fraught with danger – one false move and a turd could end up using the gusset of your underwear as a trampoline! The increasing popularity of the sit-down loo in the East probably has a lot do with the gradual adoption of Western dress.

What is Crap?

On average, faeces comprises 75-80 per cent water. Of the remainder a large proportion (estimates vary from between 30 and 80 per cent) is made up of bacteria from the gut. Faeces also contains cells that have sloughed off from the walls of the intestines, in-digestible fibre, fats such as cholesterol, inorganic salts like calcium and iron phosphates, and a small amount of protein. People who go without food for long periods are often surprised that they still defecate. In such cases they are passing a mixture of old gut cells and dead bacteria. Some turds can be described as 'floaters', and many think that this buoyancy is due to the presence of undigested fat. However experiments have shown that a more likely cause is tiny bubbles of trapped gas. Some diseases interfere with the absorp-tion of fats ('tropical sprue' for example) and can often account for the passing of greasy turds. Dietary fibre (found in bran, whole grains, beans, and some fruit and vegetables) consists mainly of carbohydrates like cellulose and pectin. Fibre is good for you as it helps bulk out food making it easier for the intestines to shift it by muscular action. Fibre also absorbs water making it less likely that your faeces will dehydrate in the colon.

Smell

The smell of some foods such as onions and garlic will affect the odour of excrement (asparagus in particular gives urine a distinctive pong) but most of the stink of faeces is due to the chemicals skatole, indole, hydrogen sulphide and ammonia. These substances are produced by the hundred or so species of bacteria living in your gut. These micro-organisms play an important part in helping you to digest your food, and particularly vile-smelling faeces are a sign that something has upset them. This is often the case with alcoholics as the booze plays havoc with the health of their tiny intestinal buddies.

Taste

(*See* Rude Toilet Behaviour, p. 205)

Colour

The colour of crap is determined by the action of bacteria on a substance called 'bilirubin', a waste product from the breakdown of red blood cells. Haemoglobin in red meat means that the crap of omnivores is commonly much darker than the green/brown droppings of vegetarians, and the droppings of carnivores such as lions are often jet-black in colour. In humans, black tarry stools often indicate intestinal bleeding. Red blood in a stool is usually due to bleeding piles.

Frequency

Most food takes between 15 and 60 hours to pass through the digestive tract: the less roughage you eat the longer it takes. In 1974 researchers found that African villagers on a naturally high-fibre diet converted food into a turd in 30 hours, while in the pupils at an English public school (on a low-fibre diet) this took three days. As a rule vegetarians have loose stools because the extra fibre in their diet helps food to pass through their system quickly and so there is less time for the gut to absorb excess water. To see how quickly food passes through your intestines eat some beetroot or a large helping of corn to act as a marker – it's a game the whole family can play!

Most Westerners dump between 100g and 200g a day (another estimate puts it at around 590kg per year), with the frequency of sittings varying considerably from one person to the next. Some people go as often as five times a day, others only once every three days. There's a record of one man who only went on alternate Sundays, and there are stories of people not going for months, or even years.

* * *

The Colon

The length of intestine leading to the rectum is called the colon. It is designed to absorb water, turning excrement from a semi-fluid to a semi-solid. This mushy mass is then shunted into the rectum by the muscular action of the colon walls. As the rectum becomes full, stretch receptors in the rectum wall stimulate a desire to defecate.

If this urge isn't acted upon, the desire passes and the waste in the rectum sometimes backtracks into the colon where it undergoes further dehydration. Should this happen too often you can end up passing some very dry, hard and painful stools.

Assuming, however, that the defecation urge is acted upon, muscular pressure forces the faeces down into the anal canal. The rectum then contracts forcing faeces out of the anus by peristaltic action. To prevent the anus from turning itself inside out, pelvic muscles help draw the anus up over the passing turd. Passing a stool can be an exhausting business. Your breathing stops as your lungs fill to push down on the chest diaphragm, while the muscles of the abdomen and pelvic diaphragm help by pushing down on the digestive tract.

In cases where the nerves controlling the bowel muscles are damaged, faeces have to be removed manually with the fingers, or flushed out with an enema.

In Sickness and in Health

The *yin* and *yang* of intestinal health are diarrhoea and constipation. Diarrhoea is caused by too much water in the faeces (over 90 per cent), and constipation by too little (less than 50 per cent).

Diarrhoea

Diarrhoea, variously known as 'the runs', the 'squits', and 'the shits', occurs when the colon is not able to absorb excess water from the faeces. This can happen either because the colon becomes inflamed through infection, reducing its ability to take up liquids, or because the food in your intestines is moving so fast that the colon doesn't have a chance to do its job. The latter occurs in people who are lactose intolerant. Lactose isn't broken down in the stomach, it enters the gut where it attracts water to form a large bulk of fluid, this bulk then irritates the intestinal walls causing them to cramp violently. This muscle action quickly drives the liquid mass through the colon and into the rectum.

Constipation

Ignoring the urge to defecate can cause constipation as the colon will absorb too much water and result in hard compact stools. A low-fibre diet can also cause problems as stools pass through the intestines more slowly and again too much moisture is drawn from the faeces. It has been known for people to become so constipated that they've had to be operated on to remove rock-hard turds from their gut.

There is some evidence that constipation can contribute to the onset of bowel cancer. The theory is that if waste doesn't move through the guts fast enough there will be a build-up of toxins produced by bacterial action, and some of these toxins might be carcinogenic.

Straining to pass a compacted turd is dangerous, as it can lead to a stroke (*see* Death on the Loo, p. 215), however it can also lead to the formation of pocket-like 'diverticula' in the walls of the gut. These diverticula aren't dangerous in themselves but, because they're dead-ends, they often become home to huge numbers of bacteria whose combined action can damage the intestinal lining. Some diverticula form as a result of hard stools pressing against the gut walls – yet another reason to keep regular!

Megacolon

Long-term constipation can lead to a charming condition called 'acquired megacolon' which normally results from laxative abuse. Rather than change their diet some constipation sufferers habitually use laxatives to try and get things moving. However long-term laxative use can numb the walls of the gut. As a result the colon can no longer move faeces by muscle action and it gradually starts to fill, sometimes ballooning to a grotesque size. Surgery is often the only answer. Elvis may have been suffering from something similar when he croaked on the lavatory (*see* Death on the Loo, p.215).

Haemorrhoids

Also known as 'piles' haemorrhoids are veins in the rectum that become enlarged due to high blood pressure in that area. Straining increases blood pressure as does pregnancy and standing upright for long periods. Two sets of veins can suffer: internal veins in the lower rectum and external ones around the anus. Most haemorrhoids are harmless unless a clot forms in them in which case they become inflamed and itchy. Internal haemorrhoids may also start bleeding, or protrude through the anus, if they are rubbed against or dragged down by a large hard stool. If haemorrhoids become very uncomfortable they may have to be whipped out surgically.

IBD

Inflammatory Bowel Disease (IBD) is a blanket term for two ghastly conditions called 'ulcerative colitis' and 'Crohn's disease'. The latter involves the inflammation of any part of the digestive tract while the former only attacks the rectum and colon. Since inflammation inhibits water uptake both conditions can cause severe diarrhoea. IBD seems to be a genetic disorder and in severe cases of intestinal ulceration surgery may be necessary to remove the rectum and colon. If this happens the severed end of the gut is attached to a hole in the abdomen (a colostomy) and faeces is collected in a colostomy bag.

Welcome Guests

BACTERIA

There are billions of bacteria and other microscopic organisms living in your gut and they do a very useful job helping to break down your food. In fact most vitamin K and B-complex vitamins are derived from the action of bacteria. One of the bacteria commonly found in the gut is *Escherichia coli*, otherwise known as E. coli. This is a friendly and industrious little bacterium that does a lot of good work. Sadly it has an evil twin called E. coli O157:H7, a bacterium gone bad which causes intestinal haemorrhaging by attacking the lining of the gut wall. For most people it is little more than an annoyance, but in the very young and the elderly, it can be fatal. In 1998 a serious outbreak of E. coli O157:H7 in Scotland resulted in 160 poisonings and 20 fatalities.

Unwelcome Guests

ROUNDWORMS

There are hundreds of species of roundworms, some of which are parasitic to humans. Those that live in the human gut generally interfere with the uptake of fats and proteins, and if present in large numbers can cause a blockage necessitating surgery.

Two common types of roundworm are 'hookworms' and 'threadworms' (also known as 'pinworms').

The eggs of hookworms hatch out in warm wet soil. The larvae then find their way into your gut in one of two ways. Either they are eaten in contaminated food or water, or they take the scenic route: this involves being trodden on, burrowing through the skin of the foot, travelling to the lungs via the bloodstream, burrowing from the lungs to the throat then being swallowed. Hookworms are relatively large and serious infections can occur when more than a hundred adult hookworms crowd into your intestines.

Threadworms/pinworms spend most of their time in your gut. Mature females migrate down your back passage in the night and lay eggs on the skin surrounding the anus. The eggs are then shed onto clothing, bed linen, fingers etc. and some are accidentally eaten. Understandably a symptom of threadworm infestation is a very itchy bottom.

TAPEWORMS
These are picked up through infected meat containing tapeworm larvae. They inhabit the gut but usually only

cause serious problems if they get so large that they form an obstruction. Adult tapeworms can sometimes cause anaemia, diarrhoea and weakness, but are only lethal if you happen to swallow their eggs rather than their larvae. In this case the eggs hatch in your gut and the larvae travel all around the body. As a result worms can develop in every organ of your body (including the brain, for example) usually with fatal results.

AMOEBA

There are many helpful amoeba living in your gut, but one type, *Entamoeba histolytica*, is responsible for amoebic dysentery. These amoeba attack the mucus lining of the gut creating large bleeding ulcers. During the Second World War, General Montgomery had a lot to thank amoeba for when most of Rommel's senior officers had to be airlifted from the El Alamein battle-field suffering from amoeba-induced squits.

GOOD WORMS?

Some researchers believe that intestinal worms might be good for you. They claim that humans have been living with worms for so long that the body has adapted to cope with their presence. If you take away the worms your immune system is thrown out of kilter. In the USA some sufferers of Inflammatory Bowel Disease were given the eggs of parasitic worms to drink and most went into remission in a matter of weeks.

Toilet Diseases

Despite belief to the contrary it's very hard to catch diseases from toilets. Cases of hepatitis, dysentery, a number of fungal diseases, and at least one case of syphilis *have* been traced to loo seats, but in principle you are only at risk if you have broken skin on your backside. A seat splattered with fresh urine should be safe as urine is sterile (although you'd probably want to wipe it down anyway), and thankfully the toilet seat is a harsh and inhospitable place for bacteria.

Surprisingly you are more at risk from the air in a toilet than from the seat itself. Experiments have shown that flushing produces a fine 'aerosol' of toilet water that can spread bacteria around the room. Closing the lid doesn't help since it is not airtight and the aerosol simply squirts out from around the edges, usually travelling further than if the lid was left up.

Another area of risk is toilet paper. The old hard, shiny 'medicated' paper used in Britain until the 1960s was an effective barrier between your anus and your fingers, but this is not true of soft, absorbent paper. The same qualities that make soft paper so comfortable to use also allow some bacteria to sneak through if you don't use a thick enough wad. As the cover says, 'Now Wash Your Hands!'

In fact, the most likely area to harbour germs is the main toilet door (particularly in the case of large public conveniences). Everyone touches this door when coming in or going out and there are always some people who don't wash their hands before doing so. The more fastidious are advised to open these doors surgeon-style, with the elbows.

Typhoid

In the past, typhoid fever was often confused with 'typhus', a disease with very similar symptoms. However, the latter is passed on by lice while typhoid is the work of a *Salmonella* bacillus. In built-up areas typhoid germs were passed on through drinking water contaminated by seepage from cesspools. The disease's most famous victim was Prince Albert who died from it in 1861. Another victim was writer Arnold Bennett who died in 1931 after drinking Parisian tap water to demonstrate to friends that it was safe!

Mary Mallon (otherwise known as Typhoid Mary), was another typhoid celebrity. A cook who lived in New York and Massachusetts at the turn of the 20th century, Mary had the disease, but suffered no ill effects, and acted as a carrier, passing it on through her home-made ice cream. Official statistics blame her for 53 cases resulting in three fatalities, however there is also some suspicion that she may have been responsible for the 1903 outbreak in Ithaca that resulted in

1400 cases. Not surprisingly Mary was quarantined for life once her role was discovered.

CHOLERA

Caused by the bacillus *Vibrio cholerae*, cholera is the most impressive of all toilet diseases, responsible for hundreds of thousands of deaths worldwide. It originated in the East and spread to Europe via returning travellers, the first recorded outbreak in England being in 1831 in the town of Sunderland. A year later America had its first outbreak in New York.

Cholera is passed on either by physical contact or through drinking water that's been contaminated by the faeces of a victim. During an epidemic there's usually plenty of faeces around as the disease's main symptom is violent diarrhoea. Though not always fatal, death often follows within 12-48 hours of the disease's onset. Cholera can strike astonishingly quickly – one survivor of the 1832 epidemic in New York described how he was walking down the street apparently quite healthy when he suddenly collapsed as if he'd been struck by an axe.

For years few people had any idea that the disease was spread though drinking water, and it wasn't until 1854 that Dr John Snow, a Yorkshireman residing in London, showed statistically that sewage-contaminated water was the most likely culprit.

Bowel Health

People have been obsessed with emptying their guts for centuries. For obvious reasons faeces have been considered 'unhealthy' and most people are anxious to get rid of theirs as quickly as possible. One famous experimenter in the field of bowel heath was the Victorian doctor, John Harvey Kellogg, who wrote a book about colonic hygiene. According to Dr Kellogg the slow passing of stools led to the build-up of poisons in the gut and it was every person's duty to defecate at least four or five times daily. It took, he said, 40 hours for food to pass through the gut but with his therapy this time could be reduced, he claimed, to a healthful two hours.

In the late 19th century Dr Kellogg set up the Battle Creek Sanitorium where he developed a number of unusual bowel treatments. To help his patients defecate at the required frequency he had cannonballs rolled on their abdomen, their anuses were stimulated with dumbbell-shaped vibrators, and they were given frequent enemas. Visitors to his sanatorium were often put on special diets to encourage regularity. One all-milk diet consisted of 6 quarts a day, to be drunk at half-hourly intervals. The doctor was particularly vociferous against meat-eating and claimed that Englishmen had sallow complexions and bad breath because of their taste for beef.

Today the name Kellogg is synonymous with the famous cereal company, but it was actually Dr Kellogg's brother, William Keith Kellogg, who deserves the credit for the family cereal connection. Pre-cooked cereals were initially developed by a group of Seventh Day Adventists who set up shop in Battle Creek in the 1860s. Being strict vegetarians they developed a rudimentary cereal product for their own use. Dr Kellogg then developed a similar cereal (a kind of baked and ground wholemeal dough) for his sanatorium patients. One patient, a businessman called C.W. Post, saw the huge potential of cereals, invented yet another cereal called 'Postum' and started manufacturing it on a large scale. These 'healthful' pre-cooked foods became something of a national craze and William Keith Kellogg jumped on the bandwagon launching the 'Battle Creek Toasted Corn Flake Company' in 1894, the company now known as Kellogg's. Hundreds of others followed in his footsteps and Battle Creek became known as Cereal City.

Enemas and Clysters

Enemas have been popular as bowel cleansers since the days of ancient Egypt; even the Romans enjoyed the occasional squirt of seawater up the bum. An ordinary enema flushes water into the rectum whereas more comprehensive ones flood the rectum and colon in a process known as colonic irrigation. In both cases the object is to thoroughly cleanse the gut by flushing away impacted faeces clinging to the intestinal walls.

Clysters are similar to enemas but the fluids used for flushing have supposed curative properties. Traditionally the French have always been very partial to clysters and used them to administer medicines. One 19th-century French remedy for fainting women involved blowing invigorating tobacco smoke up their backsides – an activity which would wake up most people. Some people even tried a mixture of medicine and religion – the Duchess of Alba attempting, unsuccessfully, to save her son's life with a clyster of powdered Saints relics!

In the reign of James I a hanged man was kept alive with food clysters after the rope crushed his throat but failed to throttle him, while in 1613 Sir Thomas Overbury was actually murdered via his back passage. Sir Thomas's enemies at Court first sent him a number of poisoned tarts and jellies then, presumably after he'd consulted a doctor about stomach pains, arranged for him to be given a clyster containing a sublimate of mercury. He was soon pushing up the daisies.

Threepenny Bits

IN India sufferers from constipation were 'massaged' by being hit in the stomach by a spade.

IN AD983 the German Emperor Otto II took an overdose of constipation drugs and died of blood loss through his bleeding haemorrhoids.

ALL the turds of King Louis XIV were individually examined by a doctor, and their appearance recorded in a 'log book'.

BATH ROOM FITTINGS

Plate 1484-B.
NICKEL-PLATED TOILET PAPER HOLDER.
Price each $1.50

Will hold rolls 5 inches wide.

Plate 1486-B.
NICKEL-PLATED TOILET PAPER HOLDER.
Price each .... $

Plate 1488-B.
NICKEL-PLATED TOILET PAPER HOLDER, heavy pattern.
Price each .... $

Will hold rolls 5 inches wide.

Plate 1490-B.
NICKEL-PLATED TOILET PAPER BOX.
Price each $2.25

Plate 1492-B.
NICKEL-PLATED TOILET PAPER BOX, heavy patte
Price each $3.50

Will hold sheet paper 5½ x 7½ inches.

COLD WEATHER CRAPPING

Crapping in cold weather can be very unpleasant, especially if you're doing it in the open. An Indian tribe in Canada used to call the December/January period *kong kyaangaas* meaning 'stand-up-to-shit-month'. The cold might also be the reason why women in rural Switzerland learned how to pee standing up.

The cold can have its advantages though: a winter turd quickly freezes in the open and can be handled easily. In some parts of Greenland it was common to see turds stacked like firewood outside houses, and in Russia the cleaning of cesspits was sometimes left until the winter when they could be emptied with a pickaxe.

In the past Eskimos used to feed their excrement to the dogs. Since food was scarce in the winter months the dogs were probably glad of a hot meal. Travellers often reported having seen dogs that were so keen to fill their bellies they would try to start eating your droppings while you were still squatting. Anyone going out for a crap had to take a whip to keep the poop-hungry pooches at bay. The dogs were also very fond of urine as this was a source of salt otherwise lacking in their winter diet. If an Eskimo's dog team was getting tired they could be tricked into a burst of speed by sending someone ahead for a pretend pee in the snow. The dogs would see this activity and race ahead to get to the urine-stained snow. Apparently this trick could be played repeatedly as the dogs never figured out that they were being conned.

Reindeer also like salty urine and if you're not careful will treat you as a drinking fountain if they catch you peeing outdoors. In the past urine was often used to trap reindeer in the wild. Hunters would dig a pit, cover it with branches, then lay down a trail of piss to attract the salt-hungry animals.

In an effort to avoid the cold, dogs, and thirsty reindeer, many people preferred to pee indoors. In the 16th century a traveller visiting Iceland and Greenland recorded that people usually peed into a bottle under the table rather than brave the elements. The other people at the table thoughtfully made loud murmuring noises to drown out any embarrassing sound effects.

Anyone feeling brave enough to pee outside in freezing weather might try doing it from an elevated position to see what happens. In some countries it gets so cold that a stream of urine will freeze before it hits the ground, apparently producing an interesting 'crackling' sound as it solidifies.

Modern Cold Weather Sanitation

In chilly North American settlements some people defecate into bins lined with removable plastic bags. These devices are known as 'honey-buckets'. In larger settlements the 'Utilidor' system is often used, in which a town's hot water is generated in a central power station and pumped to individual houses in a continuous stream, much like a central heating system. Sewage pipes and cold water pipes are laid next to the hot water system to stop them freezing, and all the pipework is generally buried in an insulated wood-lined subterranean tunnel. Although effective, utilidors are expensive to build. In Alaska one recent estimate put their construction cost at $17,000 per foot. Similar systems operate in northern Russia; here the ground is constantly frozen and, as digging is so difficult, the pipework is often laid above ground.

Antarctic Crapping

There is a large number of scientific settlements at the

South Pole and, although much of the human sewage that is generated there is discharged untreated, some countries do make an effort to minimise pollution. Unfortunately the low temperatures tend to kill off bacteria that would otherwise break down sewage, so a human poo released into the wild tends to hang around for a long time.

British bases use composting toilets while American and Australian stations use regular sewage systems. To maintain a supply of fresh water these bases use 'Rodriguez wells' that pump hot water into the ice to create a reservoir of melt-water. Theoretically any solid waste that is not digested by these sewage systems is packed into container drums and shipped away for disposal.

Research scientists and mountaineers who go on expeditions across the ice have a harder time of it. All waste, both liquid and solid, has to be collected in barrels and plastic bags and dragged around on a sledge until it can be disposed of back at base.

Threepenny Bit

In England the 'Great Frost' of 1785 was so severe that the contents of people's chamber pots froze under their beds.

"Mary was so fidgety she couldn't concentrate . . .

. . . I was shocked to find that harsh toilet tissue was the ca

SCOTTISSUE—
the soft, pure white,
1000-sheet roll

WALDORF—the
soft, popular-priced,
cream-colored roll

"I WAS worried when Mary's teacher told me she was restless in school and couldn't seem to concentrate.

"When I asked Mary what was the matter she complained of an itching. I asked a friend's advice at Mother's Club that afternoon. She said it was probably caused by harsh or impure toilet tissue, and recommended Scot Tissue.

"So I bought some ScotTissue. It looked very pure and soft. In a few days Mary's trouble had entirely disappeared. I was

amazed to find that toilet tissue c so much discomfort."

EXPERIENCES LIKE TH mon. Harsh tissue can cause seriou tion. Women and girls especially, their peculiar requirements, need a absorbent tissue—such as ScotTissu

Made to the same standards of p sorbent cotton, these famous tee cleanse and dry thoroughly, safe absorbent, they assure at all times late condition. They are extremely s ing to even the most sensitive skin.

ScotTissue or Waldorf in your bat tects the health of every member o ily. Always keep a supply on h Paper Company, Chester, Pennsylv

Scott Tissues *Soft as Old Linen*

WIPING UP

Washers

Arse-cleaning can be done in one of two ways: washing or wiping. In Asia and the Middle East most people clean their bottom by sluicing it with water and rubbing it with the left hand. Conversely, eating is always done with the right hand, and in some places it's customary to sit on the 'unclean' left hand to prevent it from making any contact with food. If you do touch a dish of food with your left hand, tradition demands that you eat every scrap in the contaminated bowl.

Before the advent of soap, it was, understandably, difficult to make the left hand fragrant after an arse wipe. While water removed the excrement itself, it still left stinking digits. Rubbing the hand with earth helped to remove the smell and for this reason clods of earth were (and still are) carried by some people in case of emergencies. Small water-carriers called 'lotas' and resembling watering cans are common in some Muslim countries: these are taken into public toilets in case no water is provided on the premises. The more expensive hotels equip their lavatories with a special pipe for bum-washing while a cheaper solution is to provide a bucket and ladle. Most people in bottom-washing countries condemn the idea of wiping with paper as very unhygienic. Hindus find the idea particularly revolting, and an old Turkish nickname for a Christian is *götu böklu*, meaning 'shit-arse'.

The Bidet

One Western bottom-washing device that never really caught on in Britain or America was the 'bidet'. The bidet appears to be a French invention although no one seems sure who was responsible for it. The first mention of a bidet in print was in 1710 in which Mme de Prie, a French courtier, is said to have greeted the Marquis d'Argenson while sitting on one. By 1750 they had gained some popularity, but people still weren't quite sure what to make of them. One confused supplier advertised his bidets as porcelain four-legged violin cases. By the end of the 19th century, however, they had become very common, to the extent that manufacturers were even building portable military 'shock-proof' bidets for officers to use in the field.

Although bidets were designed primarily for bottom-washing, most Victorians in Britain assumed they were to be used for douching the genitals after sex. This gave them a risqué reputation that did little for sales.

Wipers

The Romans used a wash-and-wipe technique. Their communal loos were equipped with a sponge on a stick sitting in a jar of salt water. The sponge was for bottom-washing purposes and after use it was briefly rinsed before being placed back in the jar. Not surprisingly many Romans disliked using a 'public sponge' and carried their own. Richer Romans avoided sponges altogether and used wool dampened with rosewater.

Threepenny Bits

THE gospels of Matthew and Luke both tell of an unpleasant Roman soldier who offered Christ a drink from a sponge soaked in vinegar – unfortunately it's very likely that this sponge was of the botty-washing variety.

THE Roman historian Seneca records how in AD65 a German slave committed suicide rather than serve as a gladiator. To do this he went into a public lavatory, thrust the sponge stick down his throat and choked himself to death.

Leaves have always been used as bottom-wipers and seashells, particularly mussel shells, were popular as anus scrapers. Otherwise over the years people have used frayed rope (ancient China), stones (ancient Greeks, Muslims), balls of hay (Romans), leeks (ancient Greeks), corn cobs (rural America, the Ukraine), coconut shells (Hawaii), silk and goose feathers (the wealthy). A rule in one medieval monastery forbade the use of towels for bottom-wiping, but since some monasteries provided broken pottery shards as scrapers you can see why the monks were tempted to use something softer.

In the Middle Ages pieces of cloth were used where possible but many poor people had to use sticks as scrapers. Some public privies provided communal sticks that were carved into spoon-like arse-scrapers. These had to be handled with caution – a fact that probably gave rise to the expression 'getting hold of the shitty end of the stick'.

In later centuries the wealthy could afford to be more select in their choice of arse-wiping materials. Cardinal Richelieu used unspun hemp on his bottom, while Madame de Maintenon and Madame DuBarry from the court of Louis XIV used lace and wool respectively.

Perhaps the ultimate status symbol was not to have to clean your bottom at all: the long fingernails of the

Chinese mandarins made it impossible for them to wipe themselves – a public declaration that their bottom-washing was to be done by a servant.

Toilet Paper

As paper became cheaper, its use for bottom-wiping became more widespread. In a letter of 1747 Lord Chesterfield advised his son to use pages torn out of a good book. In this way, it was suggested, the boy would be able to improve his mind while reading on the privy then use the paper to wipe himself afterwards. Many people found this use of books objectionable, and the author Sir Robert Herrick (1591-1677) used to print the following verse in his volumes:

> Who with thy leaves shall wipe (at need)
> The place where swelling piles do breed;
> May every ill that bites or smarts,
> Perplex him in his hinder parts.

In later years people made use of scrap paper such as old newspapers or, particularly in America, mail-order catalogues. The Sears catalogue was very popular for this purpose but fell out of favour when the quality of the paper was improved in the 1930s. The new catalogues looked better but the hard shiny pages were not bottom-friendly. Apparently in parts of the former

USSR telephone directories are still used for wiping today.

It wasn't until 1857 that an American company invented paper specifically for toilet use: this was 'Gayetty's medicated paper' for 'the toilet and the prevention of piles'. In 1871 a certain Seth Wheeler patented a toilet paper perforating machine that created 5x6-inch sheets, but the perforated roll we know today was first manufactured in 1880 by the British Patent Perforated Paper Company. The company made a paper known as 'Bronco', initially sold from a London street barrow. At around the same time the Scott Brothers of Philadelphia started making perforated papers in the USA. Scott's first national brand was christened 'Waldorf' and appeared in 1899. It was reassuringly advertised as containing no 'harmful acids'. At first toilet paper was seen as a novelty, then as a desirable luxury. Many hotels found their toilet paper was being stolen wholesale and had to resort to handing over individual supplies to guests when they checked in.

The British 'Bronco' paper was made of tough esparto grass which these days is more often used to make ropes and baskets. The paper was hard, shiny, and non-absorbent, but continued to be a bestseller until the 1950s. In America soft, absorbent toilet paper (looking like crepe) was much preferred but it didn't reach Britain until the 1960s. When salesmen were sent out to push the new soft paper they used a simple demonstration to show its effectiveness: a quantity of mustard was placed on a tray and then wiped off, first using hard paper, then using the new soft paper. There was no contest.

The switch to soft paper did not win favour in all circles, the British treasury calculating that the extra storage space required by the thicker soft rolls would add £200,000 to the Government's annual toilet paper budget.

In the Communist East there were often toilet paper shortages and most people used old newspapers. In one Moscow store you could ensure a supply of loo paper by paying a weekly subscription. For this money you were reserved some rolls and informed by postcard when a fresh supply had arrived.

On at least one occasion in the 1980s Polish protesters carried banners announcing 'RIP Toilet Paper' to highlight the country's economic problems. Those dissatisfied with Communist rule tended to use the local party newspapers, or *Pravda*, while the more faithful used less disrespectful material. The old-style Communist toilet paper was brown crepe with what has been described as a 'sandpaper' surface, but this has now been superseded by toilet paper imported from the West. It's a measure of the old Soviet paranoia that even Russian toilet roll packaging had a censor's mark to show that information about the paper's origin had been cleared for public consumption.

Threepenny Bit

In the late 1990s the workers at a Moscow clock factory received a bonus in the form of toilet rolls. They were given 150 apiece and it took each worker about three days to get their stash home.

Printed Paper

Loo paper has often been printed on. In Russia the Tsar's loo paper was stamped with the imperial arms until someone decided this might be considered treasonous. In Britain all government-issued paper used to be printed with the words 'Government Property – Now Wash Your Hands'. During the Second World War patriotic manufacturers took the opportunity to print anti-Hitler doggerel on their sheets, for example 'Hitler now screams with impatience, our good health is proving a strain. May he and his axis relations, soon find themselves right down the drain'.

Some people have used toilet paper for personal revenge. The American producer Alexander Cohen once gave out loo paper printed with the name and face of his arch-enemy, the critic John Simon.

More recently, novelty sheets have been printed with jokes, horoscopes, crosswords and Xmas greetings. Some rolls have been printed as fake currency. One West German manufacturer even printed an English language course on its loo rolls. Each lesson was repeated 8 times so none of the family would miss out.

The Future

More recent developments in the toilet paper industry include 'moist paper' and 'dissolving paper'. Moist paper is designed to give you a combined wash-and-wipe effect (much like that of the Roman sponges), while dissolving paper is for use in loos that block easily. The paper is made without the use of adhesives so it rapidly falls apart when soaked.

This type of paper is particularly handy in countries like Greece where the narrow pipes of the sewage system can't cope with toilet paper. In many Greek toilets you will see a sign saying, 'Do not put anything down this toilet unless you've eaten it first!' After you've used your paper you're expected to place it in the box or bin provided. Be warned, however, as in the past unsuspecting tourists have mistaken these boxes for tissue dispensers!

Another area of scientific advance is the toilet roll holder. Over the years this simple Victorian invention has become increasingly elaborate, to the extent that today you can buy models with features such as in-built radios, digital clocks, and alarm sirens for those occasions in which you find yourself trapped in the loo.

Toilet Paper Statistics

- THE average wad of paper used for wiping consists of 5.9 sheets.
- THE annual UK market for loo paper is £600 million.
- 79 per cent of people position their toilet roll so the paper hangs down the back.
- 44 per cent of people wipe from front to back.
- 60 per cent look at the paper after a wipe.
- 42 per cent fold their paper.
- 33 per cent crumple their paper.
- 8 per cent both fold and crumple.
- 6 per cent wrap it round their hands.
- 50 per cent of people admit to having used leaves when no paper was available.
- 8 per cent have wiped with their hands.
- 2 per cent of people have wiped with a bank note.

Threepenny Bits

To assist care workers who have to wipe the back-sides of the aged and infirm, a Japanese company is trying to develop a deodorising pill that will make crap less stinky.

On inspecting the cells in an English prison it was found that one of the inmates had been plaiting toilet paper into a rope, presumably as part of an escape attempt.

When asked to describe America during an interview in the 1920s Winston Churchill said, 'Newspaper's too thick, toilet paper's too thin'.

In some parts of Asiatic Russia rural loos are provided with clods of earth for use as arse-wipers.

Thanks to rampant inflation in the mid-1990s the Ukrainian government announced that all bills worth less than 100 'karbovanet' would be pulped and made into toilet paper.

In 1991 there was a collision between two trains in Mexico. Luckily one of the trains was carrying two freight cars full of toilet paper and this helped to cushion the impact.

In 1996 the Malaysian authorities promised a crack-down on cheapskate restaurant owners who were putting loo paper on their tables rather than serviettes.

CHAMBER POTS

Chamber pots are useful devices that have been around for as long as there have been potters to make them. Some sources credit the Sybarites (members of a Greek colony founded in Italy in 720 BC, and who gained a reputation for high-living and self-indulgence) with the invention of chamber pots. Apparently they were so fond of banqueting that they took to peeing into pots and basins rather than having to leave the table.

This custom was carried on in Rome where the slave in charge of the chamber pots (the 'lasonophorus') would circulate among the guests at a dinner party offering the use of his vessel. These slaves were summoned with a snap of the fingers, an action known as the *concrepare digitos*. The tradition of 'party pots' survived into the 18th century when you could still hire chamber pots for a night of celebration. As a rule of thumb, a party's success would be judged by the number of pots that were smashed.

Urinals

There are two kinds of chamber pot, those large enough to crap into and those designed specifically for peeing. In medieval times the latter were known as 'originals' and took the form of an elongated bottle with a wide base and mouth, and a narrow neck. They were designed in this way so that people could easily slip them under the blankets on a cold night and have a pee in bed. Originals were made from a variety of materials, including clear glass to enable doctors to examine their contents. Many doctors believed they could tell a lot about a patient's health by the state of their urine. Some even claimed they could tell if the person who passed it was a virgin. This method of divination was so common that a glass original, or 'looking glass', was often hung outside a doctor's consulting room in much the same way that a striped pole was fixed outside a barber's. One successful doctor even asked for a urinal to be added to his family coat of arms.

In later years originals came to be known as 'jordans'. In Shakespeare's *Henry IV* two men complain about the lack of urinals in their room saying that they will have to piss in the fireplace instead, 'Why, they will allow us ne'er a jordan, and then we leak in your chimney; and your chamber-lie breed fleas like a loach'. It obviously wasn't five-star accommodation.

Threepenny Bit

Iɴ ancient China an unusual variant on the chamber
pot was a loaf-shaped 'piss-pillow'. This was a hollow
earthenware brick with a small hole in the top, the idea
being that once you'd emptied your bladder into it
you had a nice warm pillow-block to rest your head on.

Novelty Pots

Apart from glass, chamber pots could be made from
pewter, tin, copper, silver, gold, even lead, and from
the 18th century onwards a thriving trade developed in
decorated pots. Some were so attractive that people
mistakenly bought them as tableware thinking they
were soup tureens or punch bowls. Some members of
the nobility had their pots emblazoned with the family
crest, while others preferred that their chamber pots
had jokes or rude poems written on them. A common
joke was to paint a large eye or face in the bottom of
the pot together with the rhyme, 'Use me well and
keep me clean, and I'll not tell what I have seen'.

Pots were commonly given as wedding presents as
these 18th century 'pot' verses show:

This pot it is a present sent.
Some mirth to make is only meant.

We hope the same you'll not refuse,
but keep it safe and oft to use.
When in it you want to piss.
Remember them who sent you this.

Dear lovely wife, pray rise and piss.
Take you that handle and I'll take this.
Let's use the present which was sent.
To make some mirth is only meant.
So let it be as they have said.
We'll laugh and piss and then to bed.

Most chamber pot inscriptions were short and funny:
'For a kiss I'll hand you this'; 'Wondrous me, what do
I see?'; 'Oh landlord, fill the flowing bowl'. However,
as time went on, people began to regard these jokes as
distasteful. In the 19th century one French chamber-
pot maker was actually prosecuted for decorating his
pots with an eye and the inscription 'I See You'.

Many pots had a ceramic frog stuck on the inside of
the bowl. These frogs were hollow and, when the pot
was tipped empty, they made a frog-like 'glugging'
sound as the urine flowed through them. Other pots
doubled as 'joke' music boxes. One model, known as
the 'Patent Non-Splash Thunder Bowl', played music
when it was lifted, and a manufacturer living in the
north of England became so wealthy from manufacturing novelty pots that his newly built manor house

acquired the nickname Piss-pot Hall.

People's faces were also printed on the bottom of pots: usually a national villain like Napoleon, or an unpopular politician. In the 19th century Gladstone's face appeared in the chamber pots of many Protestant Ulstermen as he was an advocate of Home Rule. Adolf Hitler was another obvious target during the Second World War. One particular British chamber pot was called 'No 1 Jerry' and had a portrait of Hitler on the bottom with the inscription 'Have this on Old Nasty'. Chamber pots were also used for personal revenge: in 1885, dissatisfied with his progress at Harvard University, William Randolph Hurst sent personalised chamber pots to his tutors, each with a picture of the tutor in question on the inside. Needless to say he was expelled.

Conversely, pots were also manufactured in people's honour. Commemorative chamber pots were made for Queen Victoria's jubilee but with her portrait on the outside only!

Whether or not you chose to crap into your chamber pot usually depended on whether you were the one who had to clean it. People who didn't have servants to do the job for them would probably dash to the privy rather than soil a pot they'd have to wash themselves. The 18th-century writer Jonathan Swift disapproved of well-to-do people, particularly ladies, who declined to use the privy and nipped into the wardrobe to poo in a pot instead. He advised any servant presented with a soiled pot to parade it through the house and, if the opportunity arose, to answer the front door holding it.

Bourdaloues

Some pots were made specifically for women. These were generally shaped like gravy boats and seem to have been first used by the ladies of ancient Greece. In France these pots were known as *bourdaloues*, apparently named after a French priest called Bourdaloue (1632-1704) whose sermons were so long that his female parishioners smuggled bourdaloues into church inside their muffs to stop them from wetting themselves during services. Some doubt has been cast on this derivation as there are no recorded examples of its use before 1710, six years after the preacher's death. Another possible link is with *bourdallo*, a provincial French word meaning 'refuse'. Like chamber pots, bourdaloues often had internal decorations. Some had a mirror in their bottom, others mottoes like 'If only I could see', '*Aux plaisirs des dames*' ('For the pleasure of ladies'), and 'Take pity gentle maid'. Some decorative bourdaloues were made in the shape of swans or dolphins and one spectacular example by Fabergé had rubies and diamonds set in the rim and sapphires in the handle.

Close-stools

For those who didn't want to crouch over their chamber pot to take a dump there was the close-stool. This was essentially a box with a hole in the top, a pot or a bucket beneath, and usually with a lid to hide the contents of the box and help keep the smell at bay. To use one you would sit on the hole and crap into the pot or bucket below. For this reason the French called them *caises percées* or 'holey chairs'.

Some close-stools were very sumptuous: Henry VIII had one padded with velvet, trimmed with ribbons and decorated with 2000 gold nails. Many such richly decorated stools had locking lids, either to prevent others from using them, or to prevent the light-fingered from pinching the pot. Red seems to have been a very popular colour for 18th-century close-stools (in velvet or leather upholstery); however, if its owner was in mourning the close-stool might be re-upholstered in black fabric.

Royal Stools

The close-stool of Henry VIII was apparently looked after by a high-ranking courtier, Sir William Compton, known as the 'Groom of the Stole'. There is some controversy surrounding this title. Some sources maintain that the groom was in charge of the King's chamber pot and may even have had bottom-wiping duties. Others maintain that the word 'stole' refers to an item of clothing and that the groom's real function was to help organise the King's wardrobe. It's possible that the nature of the job evolved and the 'earthy' origins of the position came to be glossed over. Over the years the title has altered considerably: Charles II changed it to 'Master of the Great Wardrobe', Edward VIII to 'Usher of the Robes', and George VI to 'Groom of the Robes'. In the case of a female monarch the title is changed to 'Mistress of the Robes'.

Louis XIV had 264 close-stools in the Palace of Versailles (he was rumoured to have extra long bowels) and often greeted distinguished visitors while sitting on one; indeed it was considered a privilege to meet the King in such intimate circumstances. Louis even announced his engagement while sitting on the pot. Over 60 of the royal stools were disguised in some way, some masquerading as cabinets, chests or ordinary chairs while others were concealed inside piles of fake books. These 'book stools' were very popular, the volumes often being given apt titles such as *Mystères de Paris* and *Journey to the Low Countries*. In most wealthy households the dining rooms had pots concealed about the place for the use of gentlemen after dinner. All the prestigious furniture manufacturers of the time, including Chippendale, Hepplewhite and Sheraton, incorporated discreet recesses in their furniture in which to hide a pot.

Disposal

For many centuries the most convenient way in which to empty a chamber pot was to throw its contents out of the window. Indeed some people considered pots to be disposable and would often throw a heavily soiled pot into the street to avoid the trouble of cleaning it. The Romans had laws against throwing refuse out of windows and if you were hit by a pot or its contents you could claim damages for medical expenses and time off work. If the refuse came from a tenement the whole block could be fined if the culprit didn't come forward. These laws only prohibited daylight pot-emptying: at night it was a free-for-all and you had to take your chances.

In medieval England Richard II passed laws against the dumping of dung, and in Paris the practice was banned in 1395, however it continued unabated and most pedestrians had to keep a sharp lookout after dark. In 18th-century Edinburgh it was customary for houses to empty their pots at 10 o'clock at night. In one house at least it was the habit to empty all the pots into one barrel during the day then, at the fateful hour, fling its contents out of the nearest window.

A common warning cry when emptying a pot was *'Regardez l'eau!'* or 'Gardy loo!', meaning 'Watch out for the water!', to which you might reply 'Haud yer han!', if you were a Scotsman passing beneath. If a gentleman was walking with a lady along the pavement it was customary for the lady to walk on the inside, away from the gutter, as this lessened the chance of her getting a soaking or, worse, a turd in her bouffant.

Threepenny Bit

IN 18th-century France three ladies in an opera box caused a scandal by emptying their chamber pots on to the audience sitting in the stalls.

URINALS

In the past urine has been considered a useful resource (*see* 'Uses of Excrement', p. 171) and many public urinals were, in fact, created in an effort to harvest it. In ancient Rome stoneware *gastra* were placed by the roadside for the relief of passengers, and a similar arrangement was found in ancient China. In Japan the old capital of Kyoto was famed for its cleanliness and the refinement of its inhabitants, a reputation due in part to the large number of buckets laid out in the city streets for the relief of pedestrians. Tokyo (then known as Edo) was less fortunate, however. There, no public sanitary provisions were made and the town was generally acknowledged to be a crap-hole.

In Europe people tended to pass water wherever they felt like it, corridors and fireplaces being two favourite locations. In 1658 the French Count of Guiche even managed to relieve himself at a party by going in his dancing partner's muff.

Perhaps in an effort to discourage this random urination the French developed the *pissoir*, a men-only stand-up urinal that consisted of an enclosed waist-high screen. There was no flush, the urine simply drained away through a gutter in the floor. There are still many pissoirs to be found in France today, but they are gradually being replaced by more hygienic unisex public lavatories (*see* Public Toilets, p.101).

Germany has some distinctive urinals, for example the *cafés octagon* in Berlin. These 'cafés' are 8-sided shacks made of decorative ironwork, and painted a distinctive green. They were built as a sanitation measure when it was realised that the city's plumbing was not keeping up with its rapid growth. The first was built in 1863 and approximately 30 remain today as listed buildings, mostly in the vicinity of railway stations.

Squat or Stand

As a rule men stand to urinate while women squat or sit. This isn't always the case however. Muslim men traditionally squat to urinate to prevent splashing from 'unclean' liquid on their skin or clothing. According to Herodotus, Egyptian men squatted while their women stood, and in more recent times this custom was also observed by the Apaches of North America. It's said that the women of Kyoto learned to pee standing upright so that they could use the public urinals described earlier. This was also the best way to pass water while wearing an elaborate kimono, since squatting would only wrinkle the fabric.

In Imperial China it was thought that squatting while urinating caused kidney problems, so most people tried to stand. Some dignitaries peed through long, hollow gilded canes that deposited their urine at a suitable distance to prevent splashing their clothing.

Gents' Urinals

In 1992 a young school student from Iowa invented the 'toilet target' – a plastic target that floats in the toilet bowl and gives male urinators something to shoot at. However this is not a new idea. The WC makers Twyfords used to equip their gents' urinals with bullseyes to aim at, while others included a picture of a bee to act as a weeing target, the Latin name for a bee being *apis*. These days most sure-shot urinators have to satisfy themselves aiming at a disinfectant block or soggy cigarette butt.

An alternative source of amusement is a newspaper, some British pubs thoughtfully hanging the covers of daily papers above their urinals to act as reading matter. In Japan some urinals are equipped with small, eye-level TV sets. These are often found in the toilets of sporting venues so die-hard fans don't have to miss a minute of the action. Pubs and bars have even tried to use urinals for advertising to a captive audience.

Ladies' Urinals

There's always a queue for the ladies' loo. Although the women's lavatory usually has exactly the same floor space as the men's, a standing urinal can accommodate far more people than a sit-down commode. The women's sit-downs can also be less hygienic than the men's urinals: reluctant to sit on a public loo seat, many women will either pee squatting on the rim, or crouch bow-legged over the bowl. Behaviour which generally results in urine being sprayed over the toilet meaning it's even less likely that the next visitor will use the seat.

Over the years many manufacturers have tried to develop standing urinals for women. In 1927 the Urninette was introduced in Britain, while two American brands from the 1950s were the Sanistand and Hygeia. A more recent Dutch model is known as the Lady P. These urinals usually consist of a bidet-like bowl placed at a convenient height, but unfortunately they are often mistaken for conventional toilet bowls with hideous results.

Ladies – Learn to Pee Upright

Upright urination is a trick that few women know, however it is said to be very straightforward. According to a straw-poll on the Internet, around 70 per cent of women who tried it were able to learn the following technique:

1. Adjust your clothing so that the naughty bits are unfettered. Depending on what you're wearing this might simply involve releasing the zip on your trousers and pulling aside the gusset of your underwear. Many women are able to pee out of the zipper like a man but the fly has to be fairly long to make a hole big enough. Those with short zippers might have to pull their trousers and underwear down to knee-level. Some find it useful to press in on the edges of the zipper hole so that the labial area protrudes slightly. Skirts are held up around the waist.

2. With one or both hands make a 'V' with your index and forefinger and spread the inner lips of the vagina (the labia minora).

3. Pull back with your fingers, to lift the labia, and pee. Try to maintain a steady and strong flow of urine to minimise dribbling. Increase the pressure in your bladder when you're almost empty to jet away the last drops of urine.

97

Practise the above in the bath or shower until you are confident enough to try it in a real-life latrine situation. The advantages are manifold: you don't have to undress to the extent required by sit-down peeing, you don't have to sit on an unhygienic toilet seat, and in an emergency you can use a male urinal.

Artificial Aids

If you're one of the 30 per cent of women who can't learn to pee upright there are a number of artificial aids on the market to help you. Brand names include TravelMate, The Lady J, the Freshette, OnTheGo, and La Funelle. The basic concept is a funnel that fits over the mouth of the urethra and is attached to an exit pipe that acts like an artificial penis. They are particularly popular with outdoors enthusiasts as they allow alfresco peeing without the need to remove layers of thermal underwear.

DOULTON'S IMPROVED PUBLIC URINALS.

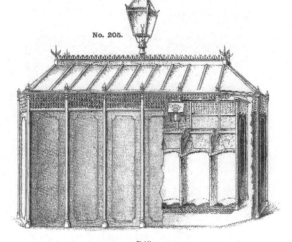

No. 205.

PLAN

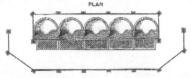

THE above design is specially adapted for narrow streets, the object being to provide the greatest accommodation in the least width.

The Screen is constructed of Slate Panels with Iron Columns, which are arranged so that a Panel can be removed without interfering with the roof or grating. The roof is made of Wrought-Iron Framing, and covered with thick glass, with a grating in the centre for ventilation and gas lamp as shewn. It may be varied to suit any position.

These enclosures are fitted up before being despatched, and each part marked so as to avoid any difficulty in fixing; and a template showing position of the holes for columns is sent with the work.

These Urinals may be had for any number of persons.

For Prices, see page 192.

PUBLIC TOILETS

Ye Olde Public Lav

The first public toilets were built by the ancient Greeks and Romans. They were multi-seater affairs some accommodating up to 30 or 40 people at a time (*see* History of the Toilet Part One, p. 1). A small public latrine dated at around 400 BC was recently excavated on the Aegean island of Amorgos. A small 7 by 5-foot structure that seated up to four at a time and served the patrons of a nearby gymnasium, it must have been quite a colourful building as the walls were decorated in red, yellow and green plaster.

In the East substantial public toilets were built. In 1556 a Mughal king called Jehangir built an enormous public toilet in the city of Alwar which is said to have serviced 100 families at a time.

We know from a crime report detailing the murder of one John de Abydon outside a common privy in London's Cripplegate, that public toilets were around in England by at least 1291. Most of these medieval loos were built over rivers or open sewers. There was, for example, a four-seater public loo near Fleet Street built on a pier, and another was built on London Bridge. At one time there were around 140 houses on London Bridge and the loo served the needs of their inhabitants – this was nice for them, but made boat travel hazardous. Rivers like the Fleet had so many privies over them they became foul beyond belief. With the onset of the Black Death the authorities began to take sanitation more seriously and Edward III passed a law banning the building of new privies over certain London watercourses. Partly as a result of this the number of public toilets diminished to the point where in 1358 there were only four of them in the whole of London.

Some enterprising people made their living as portable public toilets. In 18th-century Scotland men walked the streets with a large cloak and a bucket shouting 'Wha wants me for a bawbee?' Once you'd paid your 'bawbee' (halfpenny) you stood or squatted over the bucket and did your business while its owner shielded you with his cloak.

Modern Conveniences

In 1726 the satirist Jonathan Swift (who seems to have had a keen interest in toilets) published a 'Proposal for Erecting and Maintaining Public Offices of Ease within the Cities and Suburbs of London and Westminster'. This curious pamphlet called for the construction of grand quadrangular toilets equipped with marble statues and a central fountain and basin for hand-washing. The walls of each toilet cubicle would be painted with frescos and the lavatory seats upholstered in 'superfine' cloth stuffed with cotton. In winter the feet of toilet-users would be kept warm by laying thick Turkish carpets on the floor. Needless to say these grandiose plans weren't entirely serious.

The modern 'public convenience' saw its origins in the Great Exhibition of 1851. The pioneer of the public lavatory was an English WC manufacturer called George Jenning whose paying toilets at the Great Exhibition attracted over 800,000 customers. Many of the people who paid a penny to use his water closets were probably using one for the first time and it's thought that Jenning's experiment did much to popularise the flushing loo.

Jenning made a fortune out of his exhibition toilets and championed the construction of new public conveniences around the country; 'conveniences which nature demands and every decent man and every thoughtful mind approves'. Many towns had a selection of public lavatories but Jenning described them as 'plague spots' and pointed out that, while these privies were often demolished to spare people the sight and the smell of them, they were rarely replaced with anything better. The Public Health Act of 1848 had stipulated that public 'necessities' should be provided and Jenning's plan was to build a series of paying underground 'halting stations', each one manned by an attendant whose job it would be to provide washing facilities in the shape of a bowl, a clean towel and a brush, and clean each cubicle after use, wiping the seat with a piece of damp leather.

Despite objection on the grounds of indelicacy, Jenning's ideas eventually won through and resulted in an impressive spate of Victorian toilet construction. In fact Jenning went on to build public toilets around the world, from Madrid to Hong Kong. As one wag put it, Jenning's name was known from 'Zembla's shores unto far Peru'. The decision to build public toilets underground was made not so much to fit in with existing sewage disposal systems but to meet with Victorian propriety. It was in fact much more expensive to build these conveniences underground but the Victorians felt that the extra cost was worth it to keep public toilets out of sight and mind.

An important feature of the public toilet, the 'Vacant/Engaged' door lock, was invented in 1882 by Arthur Ashwell. The lock comprised a simple sliding bolt and Arthur later improved his design so that the bolts on ships' toilets would not accidentally slide open or shut in stormy seas.

* * *

Sadly the British public loo today appears to be in decline. Metropolitan councils have closed roughly a third of the toilets they maintain, and District councils have done the same to a quarter of the toilets in their care. While this may be annoying to members of the general public, for workers like postmen the lack of public facilities is more than a minor inconvenience, often putting them in embarrassing predicaments. To stop the rot an organisation called the 'British Toilet Association' has been formed to highlight the decline of British public lavatories. The BTA has also instigated an award scheme to reward good loo-keeping. There are various categories but the overall winner is awarded the accolade 'Loo of the Year'.

The Automatic Loo

Perhaps the most technically advanced public loo is the APC or Automatic Public Convenience. Developed in France, the APC was designed to provide hygienic vandal-proof relief for city dwellers and examples are now to be found all over Europe. On paying the fee the door opens and sensors in the floor alert the loo to your presence. The door then shuts behind you and locks automatically. Once you've finished your business (to soothing Muzak in some cases) you let yourself out and the loo automatically cleans itself: the toilet bowl withdraws into a compartment where it is cleaned, disinfected and dried, and the floor of the entire cubicle is sprayed. This comprehensive cleaning job can come as a surprise to people who try to sneak in without paying. If you slip through the door as someone leaves, the toilet will assume the cubicle is empty and give you a soaking. Apparently many American tourists are caught out this way, being unused to paying for public toilets and unaware of the APC's fiendish efficiency.

Mystery Caller

IN 1997 an elderly woman started receiving mysterious nuisance calls in the middle of the night. Although no voice could be heard, they were a source of alarm and annoyance. When the woman had the calls traced it was discovered that they were being sent by a public toilet. The computerised loo was programmed to call a maintenance engineer if it found itself in trouble, but it had been given the woman's number by mistake. The error was corrected, the loo was fixed, and the old lady was not disturbed again.

Shops and Restaurants

People are often advised when travelling to use the toilets in shops and restaurants rather than confront the often revolting public toilet facilities. In the UK, British Standard 6465 recommends that all eating places provide a toilet and suggests that shops with a sales area in excess of 1,000 square metres do the same. While these recommendations are not enforceable by law it would be very hard for a restaurant or large store to get planning permission if the loos were inadequate. Some stores like Harrods charge for the use of their sumptuous loos, a policy designed to keep out casual visitors, but many stores are starting to install toilet facilities in the belief that they are good PR and encourage visits from female and elderly customers.

Women often complain that they get fewer public toilet facilities but in theory they get more. British law states that in theatres at least one sit-down toilet must be provided for the first 250 males and a minimum of two for the first 50 females. In cinemas it is 1 sit-down toilet for the first 100 males and 2 for the first 75 females. As it happens most people will visit a public toilet to have a pee and only the male loos are equipped with urinals; these have a fairly rapid turnover of customers hence the lack of queues outside the gents (*see* Urinals, p. 93).

Ladies and Gents

It's not certain when public toilets were first divided into 'Ladies' and 'Gents'. The first might have been a 'long house' built over a Thames inlet in the 15th century by Dick Whittington, the Lord Mayor of London. The house provided seating for 64 men on one side and 64 women on the other. In 1729 Jonathan Swift built 'his and hers' toilets for his friend Lady Acheson (as he put it, 'in sep'rate cells the He's and She's here pay their vows with bended knees'). However, according to most sources, the first 'modern' public division was in 1739 when a Parisian restaurant provided separate ablutions for the patrons of a large dance party.

The most common way of distinguishing toilets is to label them 'Gentlemen' and 'Ladies' or to use stylised 'male' and 'female' outlines; however there are many other ways to do it. In some parts of the world a circle represents women while men are an inverted triangle. One New York bar has pictures of dogs on the toilet doors, the men being represented by a pointer, and the women by a setter. Another in London has bulldogs and poodles. In a similar vein some toilet doors in 'nautical' pubs are labelled Gulls and Buoys. Other examples are Ducks and Drakes, Stags and Does, Derbys and Joans, Studs and Fillies, Guys and Dolls, Barneys and Wilmas, Nuts and Bolts, and so on.

In Latin countries hotel toilets are often labelled '100', so when enquiring as to the whereabouts of the lavatory you need to ask for *numero cento*. It's not certain why this should be, but it's been suggested that the name might have originated in Victorian times when British travellers marked the toilet door with the word 'loo' to assist their fellow countrymen. Hoteliers might have confused the letters for numbers and assumed this was the correct labelling.

Chemical Toilets

Although chemical loos are found in a number of locations (boats and caravans) most people are familiar with them as makeshift public conveniences. In Britain the most famous brand of chemical toilets is Elsan, founded by E. L. Jackson in the 1920s (the name is a combination of the initials, E. L. and 'san' as in sanitation). These early toilets were basically buckets containing a pool of blue disinfectant. Today there are a number of models to suit every occasion. The more sophisticated ones are flushable, the waste being deposited in a leak and odour-proof portable container resembling a suitcase.

Festivals

Many people's experience of public toilet facilities will have been at a fête, rally or festival. The toilets at the Glastonbury Festival are notoriously vile. In the festival's early days a loo at Glastonbury consisted of a ditch with two scaffolding poles slung over it to provide a seat and/or footrests for squatting. These days the site is equipped with slightly more sophisticated 'box latrines' based on the trench latrines used by the army (*see* Military Loos, p.139). Theoretically these trench toilets are completely enclosed but this doesn't prevent a number of drink and drug-addled toilet users from falling down them (or being pushed into them) each year.

To cope with sanitation demands these trench toilets are now often supplemented by a number of chemical Portaloos. Using these can be a hazardous experience as festival-goers with an 'impish' sense of humour have been known to wait until one is occupied then push it over, doorside down if possible.

Threepenny Bits

THE Greek philosopher Diogenes used to say there should be no distinction between public and private life. To make his point he once crapped in the local market place.

ON average men will spend 45 seconds in a public toilet cubicle. Women spend 80 seconds.

DURING the 1980s approximately 20 people a year died in the public toilets of Westminster.

IN the 19th century New York's Central Park was equipped with a hundred 'earth closets'.

IN New Jersey, handbag thieves would reach into ladies' toilet cubicles and steal bags hanging on the door-hooks. To solve the problem the police removed the hooks. The thieves put up new ones.

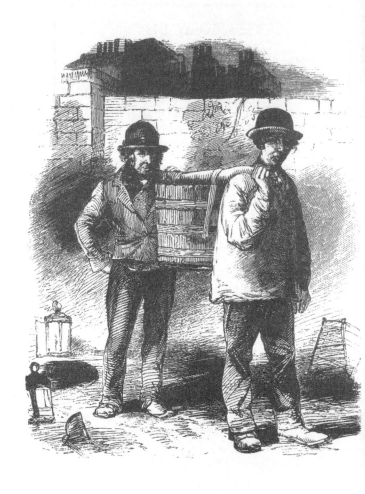

CESSPITS

The Cesspit in History

For centuries most household sewage was gathered in cesspits, otherwise it ended up in the streets or the nearest river. In many medieval cities there were strict rules about the construction of these pits. In 1189 Henry Fitzalwyn, the first Lord Mayor of London, decreed that any 'necessary chamber' built of stone had to be situated at least two and a half feet from a neighbouring building, or three and a half feet if it was made of wood.

It was important to line a cesspit to prevent it from collapsing. In one Viking settlement a pit was found lined with branches; this might have been the site of an early privy. These cesspits were not watertight, the idea was that liquid would slowly seep into the surrounding soil while the solids would either break down naturally or be shovelled out.

Sewage breaks down aerobically in the presence of oxygen and anaerobically in airless conditions. The anaerobic digestion of sewage by micro-organisms is slow and produces stinking gases like hydrogen sulphide. Few medieval cesspits had any sort of ventilation and their contents might stew in the darkness for years. In many areas this situation continued well into the Victorian period, when the popularity of water closets and the volume of waste water they produced forced planners to build modern sewage systems.

Some cesspits were built in odd, irregular shapes and children were often employed to clean the smaller crannies. As a result legislation was introduced in Victorian times to ensure that no new cesspit was to be built that could not be emptied by an adult.

Although the job of emptying a cesspit was unpleasant, it was well paid. A Victorian night-soil man (in earlier times known as a 'gongfermor' or 'raker') could expect to be paid a shilling a pit in an age when three shillings a day was a good wage. The sewage sludge could also then be sold to bring in extra money. Sewage was used in agriculture as fertiliser and in the munitions trade as a source of nitrates. Unfortunately the value of sewage dropped to nothing after the 1850s as guano fertiliser became cheaper and gunpowder manufacturers discovered better nitrate sources. As a result many night-soil men began to illegally dump their unwanted sewage in rivers, waste grounds and back alleys. To make up their wages they also put up their prices and many poorer families allowed their cesspits to overflow rather than pay the extra money.

An unventilated cesspit could be a dangerous place. An official report of 1849 reads as follows: 'The smell was of the most horrible description, the air being so foul that explosions and choke damp were frequent. We were very nearly losing the whole party by choke damp, the last man being dragged out on his back through two feet of black fetid deposit in a state of insensibility.' It could be just as dangerous living above a cesspit as its reeking fumes would often rise up and invade a house. Oddly enough more people were worried by industrial pollution. It was believed that sooty and sulphurous 'night air' was particularly dangerous and in the evening houses were sealed to prevent it from entering the house. This often precluded the venting of rising cesspit fumes and it was not uncommon to find entire families suffocated by sewer gases. Explosions were also frequent occurrences. Rotting sewage produces methane and if these gas pockets were disturbed by someone holding a naked flame the consequences could be dire.

The Cesspit Today

Cesspits (or cesspools) are not a thing of the past. In modern America approximately 60 million people use one, and most isolated communities worldwide depend on them, the only alternative being a composting toilet.

Strictly speaking, a modern cesspit is a watertight holding tank for sewage and waste water. No leakage is allowed, the pits have to be emptied regularly and their contents removed to a sewage plant. It's been estimated that an average person produces 100-150 litres of effluent per day and in the UK the minimum capacity of a cesspit is 18,000 litres.

The cesspit's cousin is the 'septic tank', usually a large chamber that accepts household sewage and often all domestic 'grey water', i.e. the dirty water from your sink, shower, bath, washing machine, and so on.

The septic tank relies on anaerobic bacteria to digest solid waste, breaking it down into gases and liquid. When sewage enters a tank the solid waste settles to the bottom. As the tank fills, the liquid waste seeps out into the soil via an outflow pipe. Since anaerobic digestion is inefficient, septic tanks have to be cleaned out once in a while. Some large tanks can be pumped empty every three years but in the UK it is recommended that they are 'desludged' every 12 months. If tanks are not cleaned regularly the solid matter will build up until it slops over into the seepage system and blocks it.

To improve seepage, septic tanks are often equipped with 'leachlines' or 'seepage pits'. Leachlines are long perforated pipes that help to distribute liquid from the outflow pipe, while a seepage pit is usually a deep 'well' made from concrete rings piled on top of each other. Distribution of waste water helps to clean it as aerobic bacteria living in the soil break down any sewage particles that might still be floating around. The process is very similar to the organic cleaning system used in some sewage treatment plants (*see* Composting Crappers, p. 119).

CRAPPER'S

Improved

Registered Ornamental

Flush-down W.C.

With New Design Cast-iron Syphon Water
Waste Preventer.

COMPOSTING CRAPPERS

In many situations it's impossible to connect a house to a sewage system and in these cases you can either dig a cesspit or obtain a composting lavatory. Some people deliberately choose composting lavatories because they are 'eco-friendly'.

In developed countries a huge amount of treated drinking water is used to flush waste; in fact about 40 per cent of the water piped into a modern house disappears down the toilet. Added to this wastage is the problem of disposing of sewage sludge from treatment works.

Sewage Treatment

In a modern treatment plant, sewage is first filtered to remove large objects like nappies, panty liners and dead pets. It then goes to a large settling tank where it is allowed to sit for a few days. Solid matter makes up only around 2 per cent of raw sewage and this settles to the bottom of the tank to form a layer of sludge. The dirty water at the top of the tank is then drained off and sprayed over organic filter beds. These beds are home to a thriving community of micro-organisms that break down any organic matter remaining in the water. After going through a number of filters the clean water is then pumped into a waterway.

The sludge that's left presents more of a problem. It is extremely noxious, stinks, and is not much good for anything. Some sewage plants sell sludge to farms as fertilisers but in many cases it is contaminated by toxic waste from factories. Most sludge is dumped at sea, buried in landfills, or burnt. Not surprisingly centralised sewage treatment is very expensive. It's been estimated that in the near future the US Federal Government will be spending around $7 billion a year on sewage projects.

Composting toilets side-step many of these problems: they use little or no water so there is less waste, and the composted sewage can be shovelled on to the garden.

How Sewage Rots

Left to its own devices faeces tends to decay 'anaerobically'. Anaerobic digestion is very slow and produces gases that are both inflammable and smelly. In addition, many of the anaerobic bacteria involved in this decay are harmful to humans.

If sewage is exposed to air its decay becomes 'aerobic'. The bacteria involved in aerobic decay are 'thermophiliic' (i.e. they like heat), they break down sewage into carbon dioxide and water and release energy in the process. The heat generated can be quite fierce and it usually destroys any nasty anaerobic bacteria lurking in the vicinity.

In one test aerobically composted excrement was found to contain 40 anaerobic bacteria per gram, the 'safe' level is 200 per gram, and untreated sewage sludge typically contains 100,000 per gram.

In many cases the heat generated by thermophilic bacteria can be harnessed for use in the home. Some ecologically minded people with a flair for DIY have built heat exchangers to extract energy from rotting manure, using it to provide a household with hot water. Theoretically it would be perfectly possible to make an 'organic hot tub' by installing a suitable bath in the middle of a well-composted dung heap.

Composting Your Crap

Composting toilets usually contain a chamber primed with a 'soak' consisting of a layer of wood shavings or sawdust. The soak provides bacteria with a source of carbon, and mops up excess fluid allowing the excrement to become aerated. These wood particles also provide a large surface area for aerobic bacteria to work on. Ventilation pipes maintain a steady supply of oxygen and aeration is assisted by regularly stirring up the mixture. These toilets may also be heated to encourage the growth of aerobic bacteria. Some composting toilets are so efficient that they can even cope with food scraps and grass clippings.

Bioloos

Toilets that compost faeces are often known as 'bioloos'. The user sits on a toilet seat and defecates into a plastic bin primed with a soak. After they've finished, the faeces and soak are stirred by revolving mixer arms. This might be done manually or there might be an electric motor to do it for you. Used frequently these loos could need emptying once a week, otherwise they might not need attention for months.

A popular brand of bioloo is the BioLet. These toilets have a nice refinement in that the composting bin is hidden from view by a sliding plastic tray. When you sit down the tray withdraws automatically allowing you to do your business.

Composting Chambers

A well-known Swedish brand of bioloo is the Clivus Multrum. Here a 'no-flush' or 'low-flush' toilet is situated in an upper room directly above a sewage chamber installed in the basement. When you assemble your chamber you have to be careful to pack the soak material into a slope, as tumbling excrement down this incline helps to break it up and aerate it. The composting process is continuous and mature sewage is periodically shovelled out of a hatch. Although the Clivus Multrum uses fan-assisted ventilation, it has no mixing blades. Instead special 'Composting Worms' are sent to you by mail to be dropped into the chamber. These worms (*Eisenia foetida*) tunnel through the sewage, churning it up and aerating it as they as they go. Since they actually eat the sewage they also help to reduce its mass considerably. However, you do have to be careful not to put strong chemical cleaners down the loo, as these might kill your worms and land you, quite literally, in deep shit.

There's a great demand for composting toilets in Scandinavia as many people live in isolated communities that cannot be plumbed into a regular sewage system. Apart from the difficulties of laying sewage pipes in Sweden's rocky landscape, the freezing winters would soon destroy most rural sewage networks. In the Norwegian town of Tanum the local council has gone as far as declaring war on the flush toilet. People wishing to connect their new homes to the sewage system have to pay over £3000 for the privilege and the adoption of composting toilets in older houses is actively encouraged. All the composted sewage is gratefully received by local farmers.

The Earth Closet

Cousin to the composting toilet is the 'earth closet' invented by a Victorian vicar called Henry Moule. The Reverend Moule thought that cesspits were an unnatural abomination and had those in his house filled in. Thereafter he and his family went in buckets, the waste being buried in the garden. While burying some crap in the flowerbeds the Reverend realised he was digging in an area that had already been used for sewage disposal, however to his surprise there was no trace of any previous poop deposits. Moule did some experiments and discovered that a mixture of sewage and dry soil was inoffensive both to the eye and nose. Encouraged by this, he went into business around 1860 and started the Moule Patent Earth Closet Company Ltd. The Moule closets worked like water closets but the flush was a shower of dry earth released from a hopper. Once used, the earth/poop mixture could be dried and recycled six times before it had to be disposed of.

Earth closets were very popular for a time; many schools installed multi-seater earth closets and Queen Victoria had one in Windsor castle. Their main drawback was the amount of time it took to dry and prepare the soil. This wasn't a problem if you had servants to do the job, but earth closets gradually disappeared as the wages of domestics increased.

The DIY Grow-Bag

In Africa most people defecate in primitive pit toilets (*see* Crappers of all Nations, p. 159), however there's always a risk that these loos might contaminate the groundwater and they're a waste of valuable fertiliser. To try and recycle these nutrients, scientists and aid workers in Zaire are experimenting with 'grow-bag' latrines. To use them, people defecate into a black plastic sack, then sprinkle soil over each deposit to deodorise and compost it. Once the bag is half full it is tied off, punctured with a stick, and planted with seeds. The bag is then buried in a vegetable patch. The human compost helps trap moisture and provides the sprouting vegetables with yummy nutrients.

DOULTON'S IMPROVED SEATS

For PEDESTAL "SIMPLICITAS" CLOSETS.

No. 150.   No. 150A.

No. 150B.   No. 150C.

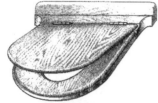

No. 150E.

SECTION. No. 150E.

PRICES.	Pine.	Polished Pine.	Mahogany.	Walnut.	Teak.
	£ s. d.	£ s. d.	£ s. d.	£ s. d.	£ s. d.
No. 150.—Pedestal "Simplicitas" Closet Seat, - each,	0 13 6	0 17 0	1 1 0	1 1 0	1 1 0
No. 150A.—Do., do., with Paper Box, - „	0 15 0	0 18 6	1 4 0	1 4 0	1 4 0
No. 150B.—Do., do., „ Hinged Flap, - „	1 1 0	1 7 6	1 15 0	1 15 0	1 15 0
No. 150C.—Do., do., with Hinged Flap and Paper Box, „	1 4 0	1 10 0	1 17 6	1 17 6	1 17 6
No. 150E.—Do., do., with Self-lifting arrangement, - „	1 5 0	1 11 0	1 15 0	1 15 0	1 15 0

No. 150D.—Cheap Mahogany Seat, as No. 150, in single thickness, with Back Rail same width as seat, 15/-.

All Seats with the exception of No. 150D. are made in double thickness.

TRANSPORT TOILETS

Railway Loos

In Britain it took a surprisingly long time for toilets to be installed on trains. The rail companies modelled their service on the stagecoaches they replaced and, since coaches didn't have on-board toilets, it didn't occur to anyone to put one in a carriage. There was also the question of cost; early trains didn't have corridors and it would have been expensive to give each carriage its own WC. In 1850 the South-Eastern Railway Company built a 'Royal Saloon' carriage with a commode hidden inside a sofa, and other companies soon came up with similar arrangements. Saloons equipped with toilets were usually meant for invalids; everyone else had to hang on until they reached a station with a loo stop (in some cases these stops were marked with a 'z' in the timetable). In the 1880s WCs started appearing on ord-inary trains, a toilet compartment being shared by the carriages on either side of it. Trains with toilets reached by a side-corridor became common only in the 1890s.

In America, rail journeys were usually much longer than those in Britain and, as a consequence, US trains were fitted with toilets as early as the 1830s. These were fairly primitive affairs, the toilet compartment being a tiny wooden cupboard containing a seat over a hole in the floor.

Indian Railway Loos

The following is a copy of a letter sent to a Railway Superintendent in West Bengal in 1909. It graphically describes the inconvenience of station toilet stops.

Dear Sir,
I am arrive by passenger train at Ahmedpore station, and my belly is too much full of jack fruit. I am therefore went to privy. Just as I doing the nuisance, that guard making whistle blow for train to go off and I am running with lotah in one hand and dhotie in the next hand. I am fall over and expose my shockings to man, females, woman on platform. I am get leaved at Ahmedpore station.

This too much bad, if passenger go to make dung, that dam guard no wait train 5 minutes for him. I am therefore pray your honour to make big fine on that

guard for public sake, otherwise I am making big
report to papers.
your faithful servant
sd./ Okhil Ch. Sen

In some undeveloped countries train toilet arrangements are still very primitive today. A traveller in rural
Thailand recently reported that the locals would squat
in the corridor, defecate on a sheet of newspaper, then
bundle up their mess and fling it out of the window.

Modern Train Loos

Most train loos originally operated on an 'open system' by which toilet waste is dropped directly onto the
track and left for nature to take care of. For this reason
many train toilets cannot be used at stations as it
results in unpleasant piles of poo underneath the noses
of waiting passengers.

Although convenient for its users, the open system
makes life stink for the track engineers. There's also a
problem with high-speed trains, in that falling crap
often hits the ground so fast that it's pulverised and
turned into a spray. This poo aerosol is then whipped
around by air currents and deposited on the outside of
the carriages (or even inside if the windows are open).
Another occasional problem is the 'reverse flow' that

can occur in tunnels. If you flush a toilet in a high-speed train as it enters a tunnel the sudden increase in external air pressure can send the contents of the toilet flying up in your face.

Hence, most Western countries now insist that train toilets operate on a 'closed system'. The waste is sucked into a storage tank that is emptied when the train is serviced. The suction employed by these 'vacuum toilets' means that they use less water to flush, commonly only half a litre is needed as opposed to the 8-12 litres needed by the old toilets.

Aircraft

The first passenger aeroplanes began flying in 1914, but patrons had to wait another five years for a plane with a toilet. The early aircraft loos were chemical toilets. They were convenient for the airline as they meant that the plane was not burdened with a heavy water tank for flushing, however they had a limited capacity and were perilous to use in turbulent conditions. The next generation of aircraft toilets consisted of a bowl with a squirt flush that emptied into a separate sewage chamber. Their main drawback was the limited number of flushes they were capable of – on long flights you just had to pray that the water supply held out until the end of the trip. This system was eventually replaced by one in which waste was chemically sterilised and filtered, the solid waste was stored, and the water recycled for flushing.

Most modern aircraft loos are modelled on the vacuum toilets found in the Boeing 767. Introduced in 1982, these loos are connected to central tanks that suck waste out of the lavatory bowls using the difference between the aircraft's internal and external air pressure. On the ground the vacuum is created artificially using powerful fans. These toilets use very little water and the waste is disinfected with a secret 'green compound'. On the ground the waste tanks are sucked empty by service vehicles called 'honey carts'.

Threepenny Bits

ALTHOUGH vacuum toilets work well most of the time they do sometimes need encouragement. If you find that your refuse refuses to budge, try laying some toilet paper over your mess and wetting it down with water from the sink. Repeated flushes should then get rid of it!

VACUUM toilets are also a source of amusement for bored cabin crew – apparently races are often held to see how fast an unravelled toilet roll can be flushed away.

Horror at 32,000feet

Vacuum systems did, in fact, exist before the Boeing 767, and a report in *Private Eye* from 1967 tells the story of one particular amply-proportioned woman who flushed the loo before she'd got off the bowl and was trapped on the seat by suction. The plane had to descend to 5,000 feet before the pressure difference dropped to the point where she could be freed. A more recent case involved a nine-year-old girl on a South African Airways flight in 1997. Like the large woman, the girl apparently became trapped by the flush vacuum and the plane had to reduce altitude to release her. The girl recovered after an operation to sort out minor intestinal injuries.

Similar stories have circulated for many years but airline officials point out that it is physically very difficult to flush an aeroplane loo without getting up first; they also maintain that the suction created at high altitudes is not very powerful.

Loo Facts

The number of loos on an aircraft varies. A recent survey found that the average number of loos in a Boeing 737 was one for every 63 passengers, but then some airlines only had one for every 102 passengers. Not surprisingly, those travelling first class get the best deal; their ratio can be as low as 11 passengers per toilet.

Experienced flight crews will tell you that loo queues are longest just after the captain switches off the seatbelt sign and just before and after meals. The best time to go is at the start of the in-flight movie.

If you think someone is hogging the toilet you can encourage them to hurry up by opening the toilet door from the outside; the plastic 'engaged' sign is connected to the latch, so by simply sliding the sign you can usually make the latch move. On other toilets the latch mechanism is hidden under a flap on the door. Rumour has it that some unscrupulous cabin crews will lock a passenger toilet from the outside to reserve it for their own use.

Bombs Away

There are many stories of people purportedly hit by frozen waste ejected from aircraft. For example, in 1998 a German fisherman claimed that he was struck by flying faeces dropped from an Airbus 320, and in 2000 a Spanish man reported that a 4kg ice ball smashed into his car. However, the fact is that the design of aircraft loos makes it impossible for them to drop waste in this way. Falling ice blocks are probably lumps of high-altitude frost being shed from aircraft wings, though this fact is of little consolation if you're hit by one.

Ships and Boats

One of the earliest records of a 'cruise' was written by a monk sailing to the Holy Land in 1480. He was travelling with a number of pilgrims, each having been equipped with a terracotta vase to pee in. Unfortunately when the weather got bad the vases were soon filled with vomit, and those passengers who were too afraid to use the ship's toilets in rough seas also used to crap in them. This antisocial behaviour resulted in many arguments, particularly as the vases were always being kicked over by people running to throw up over the side.

Things have improved a little since then. In the recent past some ships discharged their sewage straight into the sea, the waste being blown out of a seacock (a valve in the side of the ship below the water line) by a blast of high-pressure water. This could be unpleasant if the external valve jammed during flushing as the pressurised jet would blast the toilet's contents up into the cubicle.

Modern marine craft are not allowed to discharge sewage in confined areas like harbours or lakes. As a result most marine toilets incorporate a holding tank to store waste in places where dumping isn't permitted. Some of these tanks are made out of flexible material and are known as 'bladders'. Unfortunately sewage bladders tend to shift about when the boat is in motion and have been known to rupture with predictably messy results.

Marine toilets were traditionally referred to as the 'heads' or 'head' while the modern terminology is the MSD (Marine Sewage Device). The simplest type of head is the chemical toilet but more sophisticated marine toilets come in four main types: manual pump heads, electric macerating heads, vacuum heads, and gravity heads.

Manual pump heads suck in seawater through a sea-cock. The water and waste are then pumped overboard or into a holding tank. Many misbegotten land-lubbers think that just because the faeces has disappeared from the bowl the waste has been disposed of. This is not the case, and if these toilets are not pumped out properly the waste simply lurks in the pipework and festers. If you use a manual pump toilet, give it a good wash through (usually four or five pumps) to make sure everything has gone to Davy Jones' locker.

Electric macerating heads work like manual pumps but are electrically powered and incorporate a macerator that acts like a kitchen waste-disposal. The macerator turns waste and toilet paper into a homogenous purée that's easy to shift.

Electric vacuum heads use a vacuum to suck waste into a holding tank or to shoot it overboard. Since they need very little water they are designed to use fresh water from an onboard flushing tank. This is an advantage as seawater is quite corrosive and a bit smelly. There's also a manual vacuum head on the market made by a British company. Here the toilet seat is put down after use to create an airtight seal and a vacuum is created using a hand pump. A button is then pushed to release the pressure and suck the bowl empty.

Gravity heads are regular low-flush toilets situated directly above a holding tank. They use very little water but do require a lot of space.

Vacuum toilets are a popular choice on large passenger ships like ferries. However, as in aircraft (*see* above), there are dangers in using a ship's vacuum toilet. In 1986 it was reported that an old woman on the cruise ship *Pegasus* managed to flush the toilet while sitting on it. The resulting vacuum pulled out a substantial length of her intestines.

Some ships prefer to use composting lavatories (*see* Composting Crappers, p. 119) and this system has been adopted by some Royal Navy surface craft.

Container ships, though large, commonly have very small crews. To make the best use of their crew's time the ships of the Hapag Lloyd line have a glass-walled latrine on the bridge, which means that the helmsman can go to the toilet and still keep an eye out for rocks, icebergs, mermaids ...

Threepenny Bits

IN emergencies the pilots of small aircraft have been known to top up their hydraulic systems with urine.

IN 17th-century England public transport was obliged to stop if you wanted to pee. If the coach didn't stop after you'd shouted 'In pain!' three times you could go where you were sitting.

IN 1991 an American construction worker got $89,000 in compensation after suffering an industrial accident. He was sitting in a portable loo when it was picked up by a forklift truck and moved to another location.

PATENT WASH-DOWN TRITON CLOSET.

MADE IN FINEST IVORY OR WHITEWARE PORCELAIN

This ideal Closet possesses the advantages of the Valve Closet without its disadvantages.

No. 145.—Triton Closet Suite.

Attention is called to the unique form of the Improved Triton Closet, affording such great water area, and yet capable of being successfully cleansed by a 3 gallons flush. The Patent Drip Soleplate has been designed to enable the plumber to make a reliable gas-tight joint, especially with the S Trap Closet. This system, which overcomes well-known objections, is of high sanitary value, and has met with considerable approval.

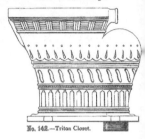

No. 142.—Triton Closet.

Patent Fire-clay Drip Sole

No. 145.—Patent Triton Closet Suite comprises—

		£
No. 8, Enamel Painted 3 gallons Cistern ...	...	1
„ 198, Cistern Brackets, Decorated...	...	0
„ 147, Bracket Pull and Chain ...	...	0
„ 139, Polished Copper Pipe...	...	0
„ 146, Walnut Seat	...	1
„ 141, Seat Brackets, Decorated ...	...	0
„ 142A, Ivoryware Closet, Decorated and best gilt	...	4
„ 143, Patent Drip Sole, fitted ...	...	0
„ 210, Paper Case, Embossed Brass ...	...	0
Price of Suite as shewn...	...	£10

No. 142.—Triton Closet in Finest Ivoryware, S or
P Trap, and with or without Vent ... 40/-

„ 142B.—Do. do. Decorated in colors ... 52/6

„ 142A.—Do. do. do. do. and picked out in best gold 87/6

„ 146A.—If with Polished Copper Buffer Plate fitted under front of seat to prevent urine trickling down front of Closet... 2/4

MILITARY LOOS

Army

Field sanitation has always been a problem for armies. If they're on the move the difficulties are not so great but once an encampment is made the resulting pile of excrement can become a serious health hazard. During the American Civil War 70,000 men are thought to have died from diarrhoea alone, and in the Second World War over 16 million man-days were lost in the US forces due to fly-borne diseases, most of them occurring as a result of improper sanitation.

Flies are the biggest problem when it comes to field sanitation. An exposed turd might be a smelly eyesore but does not become a health hazard until a fly wipes its feet on it then pays a visit to the canteen. The best way to prevent contact between faeces and fly is to cover it in some way, either with a sprinkle of earth or a fly-proof lid. Other solutions include burning waste to kill maggots, flooding toilet trenches with water or oil, or treating waste with lime or lye. Prolonged use of insecticides is a bad idea as this simply results in a population of pesticide-resistant flies.

Trench Latrines

The earliest recorded advice on field sanitation came from God in Deuteronomy, chapter 23. Here he tells the Israelites to 'go forth abroad' and 'ease' themselves in a hole (*see* Holy Shit! p. 183). God's basic advice – bury your crap – has been followed by armies ever since. Though primitive, these earth toilets still have a part to play in modern warfare. During the Balkan Conflict the British Army dug over 130 trench latrines for the relief of servicemen and refugees.

The size of a trench latrine depends how long the army is expected to stay in a particular area – in general pits are dug one foot deep for every week. While on the move infantrymen are encouraged to dig 'Cat Holes'; small pits about a foot deep that are covered with soil immediately after use.

'Straddle' or 'shallow trench latrines' are used to provide rough and ready toilet facilities during an overnight stay. Typically three feet long, a foot wide and three feet deep, they are narrow enough to be straddled by a soldier who then craps directly into the hole. The trenches are designed so that two men can use them at a time. Presumably they crouch 'bums facing' so that neither man has to watch anything nasty. After defecation the faeces are covered with a sprinkling of earth to keep the flies off. In the past many armies employed 'sanitary police' to make sure that this rule was enforced.

'Deep trench latrines' are usually 10 feet long, 3 feet wide and 6 feet deep (any deeper than this and they tend to collapse). These latrines are too wide to straddle safely so some sort of seating arrangement is provided. In the past this often consisted of a wooden frame supporting a long seating pole. This system was quite unsanitary, however, as the pole often became fouled and crap tended to smear down the sides of the pit rather than landing in a neat pile in the bottom. A more modern variation on the deep trench latrine is the 'box latrine'. Here a two or four-seater wooden latrine box is built over a suitable trench. The toilet lids are built to be self-closing and the box and pit are sealed to make them fly-proof.

Threepenny Bit

WITH the onset of air warfare deep latrines became very handy as makeshift air-raid shelters. Many servicemen have fond memories of comrades who jumped into a latrine trench rather than face enemy aircraft in the open, or confused an air-raid trench with the toilet.

Urinals

In an effort to keep solid and liquid waste separate, camps are usually equipped with 'soak pits' for use as urinals. Soak pits are deep holes filled with non-porous rubble and rubbish such as flattened cans and broken bottles etc. To keep the surface of the pits free of urine the holes are equipped with a number of waist-high pipes each with a funnel sticking out of the top. These smelly pipe and funnel arrangements are sometimes known as 'desert roses', 'piss mortars' or 'pissaphones'.

A specialised type of urinal, the 'urinoil', is a 55-gallon drum containing a small amount of waste oil. The barrel is used as a urinal, the oil floating on the top of the urine to form a barrier against flies. When necessary, the urine is drained off into a soakage pit.

Other Latrines

In places where digging is difficult, alternative toilet arrangements have to be made. The pail/bucket latrine is one in which a box latrine is fitted over a bucket, rather than being built over a pit. Again care is taken to ensure that the set-up is fly-proof.

In areas where the soil cover is thin, earth can be scraped together to form a 'mound latrine' which is large enough to accommodate a deep trench or box latrine. One can't help feeling that in a combat situation a hilltop toilet would be a rather exposed position.

The burn-out latrine comprises half an oil drum with a toilet seat stuck on the top. Sometimes a layer of lye is placed in the barrels to act as a disinfectant. More often the barrels are 'primed' with three inches of liquid fuel. Not surprisingly it's very dangerous to smoke on a freshly primed barrel. Every one or two days the contents of the drum are burned out with a mixture of petrol and diesel. Usually two drums are employed; while one is in use the other is being burned out or is cooling down. There's a story of a US soldier in Vietnam who, whether by accident or design, didn't rotate the drums in the officers' latrine and reinstalled the red hot ones rather than the cold set. It's not known if any officer's rear suffered as a result but ultimately the whole latrine building burned down.

Burning has always been a popular way to dispose of waste. In the days when armies used horses for transport, horse manure was used as fuel. As a rule of thumb one horse could provide enough droppings to burn the excrement of four men.

Modern Army Loos

In the 1990s the US Army defined a 'three-stage' latrine system that could be used in areas where traditional army toilets were not appropriate.

The first-stage latrines are known as MIDLs or Modular Initial Deployment Latrines. These are deployed alongside front-line troops and consist of a folding toilet equipped with a plastic bag instead of a bowl. After defecation the bag is sealed and stored for safe disposal. The whole unit is surrounded by a camouflaged privacy shield or tent. Units such as these were a common sight in the Gulf War where the sandy soil prevented extensive trench digging.

Second-stage latrines are called MTLs – Maturing Theatre Latrines. These are standard portable chemical toilets that have been suitably camouflaged. If the waste cannot be shipped away in a truck, provisions are made to burn the excrement on site. According to one first-hand report, these toilets are equipped with transparent roofs to allow moon and starlight to illuminate nocturnal crapping.

The third stage latrine is the FOL or Follow-on Latrine. This is a relatively sophisticated portable toilet complete with flushing system and sinks with hot and cold running water. Though complex they're designed so that two soldiers can assemble one within 45 minutes.

The Flute Loo

DURING the Second World War, a British army barracks was equipped with a communal toilet described as a 'flute', consisting as it did of a long pipe with botty-sized holes bored in the top. Running water ran through the pipe and carried away the waste.

A popular joke was to wait in the first stall (the one nearest the water inlet) until there was a full house. You would then fill a small floating vessel with combustible material and set fire to it. The vessel was then dropped down the toilet hole where it was carried the length of the toilet by the water current. As can be imagined a small burning boat travelling beneath a row of exposed bottoms and privates produced very audible results.

Tanks

As far as can be determined, no modern tank is equipped with an in-built lavatory. Tank crews ('tankers') have to get out and use the facilities provided for infantrymen. Rumour has it that some tankers (in a spirit of inter-service rivalry) prefer to defecate in abandoned defence positions in the hope that an unwary infantryman will tread in their deposits.

In the past many tanks were equipped with emergency escape hatches in the floor, and these were often used to dump waste collected by the crew. If for any reason a crew were unable to leave their tank, empty cans, shell-cases, or old helmets were used as makeshift potties and then disposed of through the floor hatch.

During the Gulf War some US tankers used the cardboard sleeves of ration packs as toilet aids. The sleeve was bent into a hexagonal tube and pushed into the desert sand to make a convenient disposable 'potty'. On the move, the same could be done inside the tank with a plastic bag held over the end of the tube.

Navy

In Nelson's navy the crews' toilets or 'heads' were situated at the bow of the ship. Heads came in various shapes and sizes but on larger ships they were a collection of holed planks positioned so that crew members could sit directly over the briney and fire away. Situating the heads in the prow meant that the following wind blew smells away from the ship and the raging sea washed away any fouling on the ship's sides. On big ships the officers used slightly more comfortable latrines situated in the ship's stern.

Modern navy loos are either composting lavatories, or low-flush vacuum toilets that suck waste out of the toilet bowl and store it in a central tank. Both of these systems are designed to conserve fresh water. Seawater is not recommended for flushing as the salt corrodes the internal mechanisms.

Submarine latrines have to use seawater to flush as subs don't have the space to store large amounts of fresh water. Submarine waste is collected in sanitary tanks that are periodically 'blown out' into the sea. Since the tanks are never blown completely empty the air used can be recycled. After filtering to reduce the smell the air is recycled round the ship, though it's said that no amount of treatment can ever completely get rid of the pong.

In the past, using a submarine loo was a complicated business. The following instructions were found in a Royal Navy submarine loo *c*. 1945. The toilet itself looked like a normal sit-down lavatory equipped with a 'gear stick' lever on the side.

To Operate WC Discharge:

1. Charge air-bottle and open sea and N.R. valves
2. Open flush inlet valve with CARE

3. Free lever and bring to PAUSE
4. Bring lever to FLUSHING
5. Bring lever to DISCHARGE
6. Bring lever to PAUSE
7. Return lever to NORMAL and LOCK
8. CLOSE ALL VALVES

What More Can You Do To Me?

AN American transport plane once touched down in Greenland in the middle of the night. The service truck was delayed and a general on board the plane became very impatient. When the truck eventually arrived an airman stepped out onto the field and started connecting pipes to empty the aircraft's latrine. The general, really angry at being kept waiting, came out to give the airman an earful. After a short but heated outburst the general threatened the airman with dire consequences if the flight was delayed any longer. The airman turned to the general and said, 'General, I have no stripes, this is Greenland, in the middle of February, and I'm sucking shit out of your airplane at 3 o'clock in the morning. What more can you do to me?' The general thought about it for a moment then boarded the plane without saying another word.

Airforce

Military aircraft large enough to hold one usually carry a chemical toilet. During the Second World War some RAF crews were apparently in the habit of dumping their chemical toilets over German cities during raids – a case of 'bogs away' rather than 'bombs away'. This practice was discontinued amid fears that the German authorities might consider toilet dumping to be an act of chemical warfare and retaliate with gas attacks.

Airborne chemical loos are only used for solid waste and, because of the smell they make, are only used in emergencies. Many large aircraft are equipped with a urinal, or carry a number of funnels attached to 'relief tubes' that vent liquid waste into the great blue yonder. Needless to say these facilities are a great source of practical jokes. Pilots have been known to indulge in aerial aerobatics when they know that a crew member is settled on the toilet, and there are numerous ways to discreetly block the pipe of a relief tube. Of course, these tubes can also block accidentally; at high altitudes urine will freeze in the exit valve so they have to be electrically heated. If the heating element is faulty it can come as a nasty surprise to whoever happens to empty their bladder first. Unfortunately poor toilet design has caused a problem in some carrier craft with overflowing urine resulting in serious corrosion of the aircraft's superstructure.

High-altitude freezing can have its advantages however; during the Second World War, American high-flying bomber crews sometimes used old ammo-boxes as emergency potties. Luckily the excrement soon froze so it wasn't too objectionable. Legend has it that one crewman suffering from diarrhoea used his flak helmet for this purpose, but put it on later when they came under attack. He only remembered what was in his helmet when the contents started to thaw.

Fighter Pilots

Fighter pilots have a harder time when it comes to going to the toilet. Few modern fighters have relief tubes, instead they are equipped with 'pee bags' or 'piddle packs'. These consist of a plastic bag containing a compressed sponge. You pee into them through a funnel attached to a length of tubing. After use the tubing is tied off to avoid leakage.

Sometimes pilots are required to wear immersion suits in case they have to ditch in the sea. In such cases getting rid of waste is a real problem, USAF immersions suits sometimes being known as 'poopy suits' for this reason. To pee wearing one of these outfits means navigating through five layers of clothing (flight suit, immersion suit, liner, thermal underwear, and regular underwear). Not surprisingly the manoeuvre can be a tricky business. At least one pilot is thought to have crashed while trying to pee and rumour has it that many have accidentally ejected themselves while wriggling about in their seats.

Obviously there can be no provision for defecation in a single-seater aircraft and pilots are fed high-protein, low-fibre breakfasts to reduce the scale of the problem. In aircraft manned by more than one crew-member, but where there is no room for a chemical toilet, it's not unknown for the desperate to strip off their flight suits and go into the nearest handy container (helmet bags are a popular choice).

Threepenny Bit

In Ancient Rome a group of soldiers felt themselves so dishonoured at being ordered to build a sewer that they committed mass suicide.

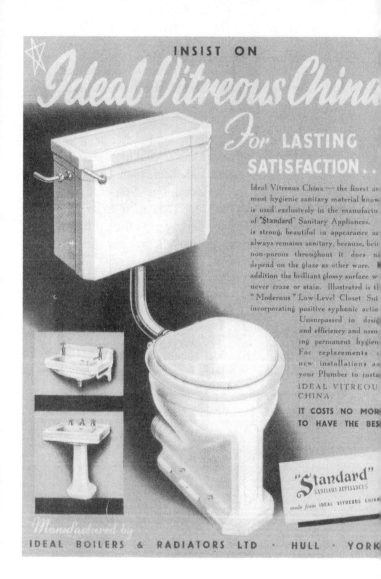

Loos in Space

The Space Nappy

The first US astronaut was Alan Sheppard who blasted into space for 15 minutes in 1961. Because his trip was expected to be a short one nobody thought to equip his capsule with a toilet. Unfortunately the flight was delayed for four hours and Alan was forced to 'siphon the python' inside his spacesuit. Since he was lying on his back the urine pooled to form a warm puddle near the small of his back.

As space missions became longer astronauts might spend between four and 20 hours in a suit which meant that the lavatorial implications had to be considered. Sadly for the spacemen the best that could be developed was a 'pee tube' and the FCS (Faecal Containment System) – basically a 'space nappy' made of elasticated non-porous material. There was a hole in the front for the spaceman's penis but the rest of the suit was tightly sealed around the waist and thighs to prevent solid waste from escaping. To try and reduce the amount of faeces produced the astronauts were fed zero-fibre diets.

The pee tube was slightly more complicated. While 'suiting-up' at the start of a mission the astronaut slipped a condom-like cuff over his wedding tackle. This cuff was attached to a rubber bladder that fitted around the hips, the connecting tube being equipped with a one-way valve. The cuffs came in three sizes, small, medium and large, allowing plenty of room for error. If a man chose a size too small the cuff would act like a tourniquet and make it almost impossible to pee. If they asked for a size too large, urine was likely to spill out inside the suit. A loose-fitting cuff also meant that it could slip off accidentally when the astronaut was moving around. Once it was gone there was no way of reattaching it.

Cosmic Commodes

With the introduction of pressurised spacecraft, astronauts were free to work in their normal clothing and going to the toilet became less unpleasant. Urination was done into a tube that used the vacuum of space to suck out the liquid and squirt it into space. Some astronauts have described the sunset dumping of urine as one of the most beautiful sights in space. Outside the ship the urine instantly freezes into millions of glittering ice crystals that stream off into the void.

A later development was a fan-assisted urinal which used an airflow to draw the urine into a collection chamber. Here a rotating separator used centrifugal force to separate the liquid from the air. The liquid was stored in a waste tank prior to disposal and the air was recirculated.

In the early days defecation was carried out using faecal containment bags approximately 6 inches in diameter and 12 inches long. One end of the bag was equipped with an adhesive flange that was stuck over the anus. Unfortunately without gravity there was no particular reason for faeces to detach itself from the bottom and cleaning up could be a very messy business. Apparently it's only in a weightless situation that you realise how much of the normal defecation process is gravity-assisted. The whole process could take easily over an hour with most time being spent trying to wipe the backside clean. After defecation there was one final chore; a sachet of disinfectant liquid was dropped in the bag which was then sealed and the disinfectant and faeces mixed by kneading the outside of the bag. This step was important as it prevented bacteria from multiplying in the faeces and producing noxious gases.

On Skylab, defecation was done sitting on a space commode. The astronauts would strap themselves onto the potty, then strain to release a turd while icy cold air-jets played around their anuses. The air jets were designed to help separate faeces from the skin which otherwise tended to stick like glue. The excrement deposited this way was then sucked into a rotating chamber containing fins that shredded the waste and deposited it as a thin layer on the inside of the drum. The drum was then periodically exposed to the vacuum of space and the faeces allowed to dry out. It was important not to let solid waste escape into space as it might have gone into orbit and collided with the spacecraft at a later date.

Modern space loos used on the Space Shuttle and International Space Station act like vacuum cleaners. While sitting on the commode you hold yourself in place using thigh bars and feet restraints. Solid waste is sucked into special bags that trap the crap but let the air through. The same thing happens with liquid waste, urine being collected in vacuum-assisted pee tubes (*see* above). When you're finished you clean yourself off with a collection of dry and wet wipes. The waste bags are then sealed and compressed before being stored for eventual disposal.

The final days of the Russian space station Mir were tarnished by problems with the toilets. Due to a financial crisis the flights of a number of supply rockets had to be cancelled, and Mir was left with overflowing sewage tanks that could not be emptied as a vital pump was missing. A week-long search failed to find the spare. The three-man crew could no longer 'flush' their toilets and the relief crew could not come on board until the problem was, eventually, solved.

SHANKS' PATENT PEDESTAL BIDET,
With Fittings for Hot and Cold Water, Ascending Spray, and Standing Waste and Overflow, comple

No. 342.

SECTION

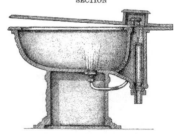

The Basin and Pedestal, with Waste Pipe and Ledges for fixing the Taps, are made in one solid piece of Por
of the very finest make, either Ivory White or decorated in Gold and Colours. The Taps are screw-down, and the W
on Shanks' Patent principle. S. & Co. have confidence in recommending this as the most perfect appliance of its
ever introduced. It is a very necessary appliance in a well-appointed Bath-room.

CRAPPERS
OF ALL NATIONS

In a recent survey, 100 travel writers were asked to rate regions of the world according to the standard of their toilets. The USA was voted tops, Western Europe came second, the countries of Scandinavia were third, and following them were the toilets of the Middle East and the former USSR. Right at the very bottom was China.

China

Most public loos in China are communal affairs consisting of little more than a series of holes in a concrete floor. They offer no privacy, paper, or washing facilities. One guidebook described them as 'dreadful beyond belief' and another advised tourists staying less than three days not to eat anything in order to try and avoid using one.

Most Chinese people have to use the public facilities as a matter of course, as many homes don't have their own lavatory. In the cities they are often run by entrepreneurs who charge a small fee per visit (about 2 pence) though the elderly, the disabled, and servicemen are usually exempt. There have been recent efforts to modernise the sanitation in China's cities with competitions held to see who can design the most hygienic and cost-effective lavatory. Unfortunately it's been estimated that, at the present rate, it would take over 100 years to modernise the seven thousand public toilets in Beijing. Some of them certainly need working on: in 1991 a poorly ventilated ladies loo exploded thanks to a build up of methane in the cesspit.

The situation is the same in rural China, where one large communal toilet may serve an entire village. Designs differ but in most cases the effluent from the privy holes slides down concrete chutes into a central sewage pit. These pits are infested with maggots that churn the excrement into a homogenous slurry. This is a good thing as far as the local farmers are concerned; the action of the maggots helps to aerate the sewage, turning it into a compost that can be raked out and spread on the fields.

There are places in China where standard Western toilets are becoming more common but according to travellers many Chinese don't understand that they should be flushed after use. Many people leave their offerings in the bowl and leave the flushing to the next in line. Singapore seems to be suffering from the same problem, although there failure to flush carries the threat of a $150 fine.

Apart from being unflushed, many of the Western toilets in China also lack seats. The Chinese are so used to squatting that they tend to stand on the seats and end up breaking them. This habit is common in Asia and the Middle East and accounts for the large number of dilapidated toilets to be found there. In some instances handles will even be added to cubicle walls to help Eastern squatters maintain their balance on Western toilet bowls.

Japan

In the past, Japanese privies were called *kaha-ya*, meaning 'river houses' as they were often built over running water. These were generally simple huts with a hole in the floor. Some were provided with an upright pole so the elderly and infirm could support themselves while they squatted. Town privies were usually built at the front of a house with their door facing the street. This made it easier for the night-soil men to come round and empty them and also meant that desperate passers-by never had to look far for a loo.

As in other countries most people used an outhouse while the rich had an indoor privy. Some worthies were assisted by servants, one to fan the face (and waft away smells) and another to wipe the bottom afterwards. Ladies had a particularly hard time as they were dressed in voluminous kimonos. There were two options with a kimono: you could either undress completely to go to the toilet, or have your servants hold your robes up round your waist. To assist in this process some conveniences were equipped with a wooden T-shaped bar to help support a lady's clothes while she lowered herself onto the pot.

The traditional Japanese loo is a squat toilet resembling a large bidet with footrests on the rim. The Japanese squat facing the rear of the loo which is equipped with a ceramic 'modesty' hood. Toilet paper is rarely provided and visitors are advised to bring their own. Visitors to Japan should be advised that public toilets are few and far between and often filthy. If you're caught short try going to a department store or visiting a café. Many tourist centres are now equipped with Western-style toilets and these are the norm in modern Japanese houses.

When using a toilet in a Japanese home, custom demands that you slip on a pair of bathroom slippers before visiting the loo. If the house is connected to a sewer then a flush toilet is the norm; if not you may find yourself pooing in a pit toilet. A pit toilet is essentially a hole in the floor over a cesspit. These pit loos can be converted into sit-down toilets by placing a 'toilet chair' over the hole – basically a Western toilet seat supported on a frame. These are popular with elderly Japanese who find crouching uncomfortable and the younger generation who are more used to sit-downs than squats.

Roughly a third of all toilets in Japan are not connected to a sewer system and are pumped empty by a sanitary worker driving a *bakumu-ka* or 'honey wagon'.

India

It's been estimated that 135 million kilograms of faeces and 900 million litres of urine are produced in India every day. Unfortunately only 30 per cent of the urban population have access to piped sewage facilities (3 per cent in rural areas) meaning that around 750 million people have to defecate alfresco. Both Hindus and Muslims are reluctant to handle human excrement for religious reasons. In the case of the Hindu population, the job is left to the lowest caste, 'the Untouchables'. As a result, the potential of human waste as fertiliser has not been exploited in an organised way, unlike in China where it is regarded as a valuable resource (*see* Uses of Excrement, p. 171).

Often, the best you can hope for in a rural Indian toilet (assuming you can find one), is a hole in the ground with a bucket of water and ladle for hand/bottom-washing purposes. Some lavatories are a little more elaborate and are flushed by a bucket of water, the excrement being channelled down a pipe that has an S-bend to create a water trap. In some cases these lavatories empty into a two-chambered cesspit. When one pit is full, excrement is diverted to the second chamber giving the contents of the first chamber time to compost.

In many parts of India men and women visit the lavatory at different times of the day. For example, in West Bengal each village will have its own recognised crapping areas in the surrounding bush. The men pay their visits in the morning while the ladies hang on till the afternoon.

Africa

The average rural toilet in Africa is a covered pit incorporating a hole to squat over. To keep out flies and wild animals this hole is usually equipped with a lid, however once the lid is removed you have to wait a few moments for the outward rush of fleeing cockroaches to subside. Once your loo is full you move on and dig another one.

Dr Peter Morgan of the Zimbabwean Ministry of Health has helped to develop a permanent rural toilet called the 'Zimbabwe long drop'. This toilet is built over a concrete chamber 15ft deep and 6ft wide. A chamber of this size should never need emptying as natural decomposition will break down the contents. A slab with two holes covers the chamber; one hole allows access for a metal ventilation pipe, the other is for defecation. The defecation hole has to be large enough to be usable by adults but not so wide that small children might fall down it. When the sun heats the ventilation pipe it draws air down through the defecation hole and through the pit. This aerates the sewage, helps it to rot, and keeps down the smell. Light attracts flies, so to keep the interior of the toilet dark (but to avoid using doors that might fall off or be used as firewood) the entrance is in the form of a spiral corridor.

Island Crapping

In tropical climes going to the toilet can be a pleasant experience, the normal practice in many coastal regions being to stroll to the beach and crap in the ocean. In the Solomon Islands it was usual for a whole village to go together. The men of the tribe would go into the waves first, followed a short time later by the ladies. In some parts of the South Pacific the islanders squat off the end of their fishing piers. Excrement makes excellent bait and having a crap often helps a fisherman to catch his breakfast.

Europe – Squat Loos

Most Western toilets are of the sit-down variety, however the squat toilet or 'Turkish toilet' is still in vogue in many places. Greece, for example, was under Turkish rule for 400 years so it's not surprising that many of its loos are of the squat variety.

Squat toilets used to be the norm in the former USSR and in many East European countries; they're also to be found in many parts of France and Italy. One traveller estimated that roughly 80 per cent of Paris café toilets are of the squat variety. Presumably squat loos have remained popular in some areas because they're robust and easy to maintain. In many cases everything happens at floor level, the flushing mechanism being triggered by a button in the ground. You should stand well back however, squat loos are notorious for the amount of water they splash around during a flush and the unwary often get soaked.

Europe and America

In the rest of Europe and America sit-down toilets appear in two forms. Wash-down closets are the norm in the United Kingdom and the USA, while wash-out closets are popular on the Continent, particularly in Germany.

In wash-down closets, excrement drops into a basin containing 3 or 4 inches of water; the flush then sluices down from underneath the rim to drive everything round the s-bend.

In wash-out closets, excrement falls onto a shallow shelf. The flush is unidirectional from the back of the toilet and undercuts any turd lying on the platform to drive it over the edge of the shelf and away into the sewer.

Many people think that the shallow ledge in a wash-out closet is an inspection shelf allowing people to examine their droppings for signs of illness. This is not the case, however, and is merely a by-product of the design. The shelf does offer an advantage in that there's no chance of 'splash-back' from a falling turd as is sometimes encountered in wash-down closets; however people unused to this shelf are often alarmed by the close proximity of their nether regions to evacuated waste.

Another difficulty with wash-out closets is variable water pressure. To work properly the flush must be quite powerful, but in places where water pressure is low (the upper floor of a tower block for example) it can take numerous flushes to dislodge a turd from the shelf. In some cases reluctant excrement has to be helped along with a nudge from a tissue-wrapped finger. In this situation, lining the shelf with toilet paper before crapping can help as it cuts down on turd/shelf friction. High water pressure can be equally problematic. It's said that if the pressure is high enough and the turd is the right shape and consistency, a powerful flush can flip your excrement clean off the shelf and on to the bathroom floor.

Threepenny Bits

IN Switzerland it is illegal for apartment dwellers to flush a toilet after 10pm. It is also illegal to urinate standing up after 10pm.

THERE is an American company that manufactures 'pot stickers' reminding men to lower the toilet seat after use.

IN India 230 million gallons of sewage enter the Ganges every day.

To help them survive the huge traffic jams of Bangkok the local taxi drivers routinely use pee bottles. One of the most popular brands is the 'Comfort 1000'.

How to Ask for the Toilet in Twelve Cities

London	toilet, loo
Sydney	dunny
New York	john, bathroom
Dublin	jacks, loo
Berlin	toilette (toy-LET-ta)
Paris	toilet (twa-let)
Bucharest	WC (vee-cheeu)
Rome	latrina (la-TREE-na)
Madrid	cervicio (ser-VEE-see-o)
Lisbon	banheiro (ba-NEER-o)
Moscow	toal-YET (phonetic)
Tokyo	BEN-jo (phonetic)

USES OF EXCREMENT

Fertiliser

Excrement and urine have been put to many uses over the years, most valuably as fertiliser. The Chinese have always used human dung on the fields and consider it a precious commodity. In fact, the worth of excrement produced in China in one year was recently estimated at around $600 million, and according to an old Chinese saying, 'Yellow gold only makes hair grow white, excrement makes yellow crops grow'. Mao Tse-tung went so far as to declare that human dung was the property of the commune not the person who produced it. In Imperial China poor people constantly scavenged for excrement; it was even imported in the form of dried cakes from as far away as Thailand. In most parts of the world you had to pay someone to empty your cesspit, but in China (and indeed Japan) the night-soil men had to pay you for the privilege. Some poor people managed to pay the rent with their droppings, however the effluent collected from wealthy families always fetched a higher price as their richer diet was thought to result in a better class of dung.

Chinese innkeepers often had arrangements with local farmers to swap fresh produce for the excrement of the guests. In Macao the excrement of visiting Englishmen was particularly prized as the English were famed as prodigious eaters who consumed a lot of meat. It was said that the leavings of one Englishman were worth those of three pigs, or eight Portuguese. Women were popular as guests because, while they crapped less, they usually defecated at the inn. Male guests were more inclined to roam and might use the privies of rival establishments if they were caught short.

Great efforts were made to harvest the excrement of travellers on the road. Shady 'comfort stations' were built by the roadside with signs inviting the weary to stop and use the pots provided.

Human fertiliser was also used in the West. In Marseilles the dung of galley slaves was sold as fertiliser, and a Victorian recycling scheme had the inmates at Cardiff Gaol producing three tonnes of manure a year to be sold to local farmers. Until the 19th century, most of London's sewage production went on the fields. Selling sewage as fertiliser was a perk for city night-soil men, and in the mid-19th century the value of Londoners' excrement was variously estimated as being between one and four million pounds. One academic put the value of an average Londoner's poop at 10s 6d a head, 3d more than was paid out in income and property tax. Many Victorians objected to the installation of London's new sewage system on the grounds that it was a waste of resources. But human sewage was unable to compete with cheap imported fertiliser and from the 1840s onwards it became harder to find a market for human manure.

Today some efforts are being made to utilise human sewage as fertiliser. During the 1970s, dried London sewage was sold as 'DagFert' (Dagenham Fertiliser) from a processing plant near Barking and more recently an experimental plant was opened in East Anglia by Thames Water. This plant operates under the name Terra Eco Systems, selling tankers of sewage sludge to local farmers. The plant also makes compost by mixing sewage sludge with straw, some of which has been sold in grow-bags. In America dried human dung has been marketed under the name Milorganite.

In the north-east of England vegetable growers were (and still are) famed for the size of their onions and leeks. Some put this down to the human manure used in their cultivation. The local toilets (called 'netties') were earth toilets that used dry soil or ash to deodorise and compost excrement (*see* Composting Crappers, p. 119). When full, a nettie would be emptied with a shovel and the contents spread on the vegetable patch.

The Reverend Moule, Victorian inventor of the earth closet (*see* Composting Crappers, p. 119) once asked a farmer to use human compost on one field of swedes and artificial fertilisers on another. The resulting swedes reared on human fertiliser grew to three times the size of their puny neighbours.

Punishment

In the days when hanging was common the prisoners' involuntary public defecation and urination added insult to injury. The stocks were another punishment that resulted in a messy pair of trousers. Being in the stocks was embarrassing enough, but to publicly soil yourself was infinitely more humiliating. In recognition of this, people guilty of lesser crimes were sometimes allowed out of the stocks for toilet breaks.

In some cases excrement was used as part of the punishment, an old Judaic law stating that anyone sentenced to be stoned to death should be rolled in dung first. The Roman Emperor Vitellius is said to have been dipped, or rolled, in dung before he was put to death, and the 'ducking pond' of medieval Europe could perhaps be better described as the village cesspool. Before a ducking the man or woman involved would often be paraded round the village on a toilet seat, so exposing their privates to public view.

The Muslim custom of cutting off a thief's hand also had an extra sting in its tail: it meant feeding yourself with your bottom-wiping hand, so that you'd be constantly defiling yourself, unless you had somebody else to put food in your mouth.

The Chinese had a particularly nasty way of disposing of criminals. The condemned man would be packed up to his neck in a barrel of lime then given lots of salty food. Once he was thirsty enough he would be allowed to drink his fill of water. Unfortunately for the prisoner, once he emptied his bladder the liquid reacted with the lime to produce intense heat so that he would be slowly cooked to death.

Fuel

Animal dung is still used as fuel in India and the Middle East but in the past dried human dung is said to have been sold as fuel in Mexico. In various parts of the world flammable methane is extracted from human and animal dung, and in Thailand an experi-

175

mental plant is attempting to turn human excrement into liquid fuel. This 'bio-oil' is created by blasting human waste with superheated nitrogen gas. The resulting fluid will apparently run a car but at present costs twice as much as diesel. In China the heat generated by decomposing dung was sometimes used to hatch eggs.

Medicine

Human urine and excrement have both been used as cures for various ailments. Sufferers of yellow jaundice were recommended to eat the dried and powdered dung of a boy who'd been fed on beans and bread. Gout was treated by imbibing the urine of a wine-drinking boy, while drinking the urine of a eunuch was said to make a woman fertile. Angina could be cured by swallowing a combination of white dog dung, human excrement, liquorice, and swallow dung. Visible cancers could be treated using a poultice of human ordure, turpentine, tobacco and dried crabs. Dried and powdered human dung was blown into the eyes to cure cataracts. In both India and Mexico eating human excrement was recommended as a treatment for snakebite. In medieval Europe it was believed that smelling faeces and drinking your own urine preserved you from the plague, and in the 18th century it was said that drinking a healthy person's urine was good for stroke victims. The Roman writer Pliny recommended peeing on your own feet in the morning as a general tonic, and peeing in someone's ear was said to cure deafness.

Beauty

Excrement was also used for personal hygiene. A mixture of sewage and donkey dung removed blackheads while in many parts of the world urine was used as a tooth-cleaner and mouthwash. The Eskimos even used urine as a shampoo. In Siberia people bathed in their own urine and used 'urine scum' as an insect repellent. It is also said that urine applied to blonde hair will have a bleaching effect and produce attractive 'sun-streaks'.

In Europe human urine was often used as a face-wash. The urine of young, healthy people was thought to be particularly beneficial and some aristocrats employed youngsters specifically to act as a source of fresh urine. For example in 1752 it was recorded that a French noblewoman employed a lusty young man for his urine-manufacturing abilities. The fresh urine would be placed inside a sealed metal container and the fluid that condensed under the lid was collected for use as a moisturiser.

Warfare

Urine is a valuable source of nitrates and as such was often used in the manufacture of gunpowder. In the Middle Ages nearly all gunpowder was made using nitrate extracted from effluent and this method was even resorted to in more recent times when other sources dried up. During the American Civil War the blockade of the South resulted in a severe shortage of munitions. To help out, wagons would tour the streets collecting the contents of chamber pots to feed the gunpowder factories.

In ancient China powdered excrement was sometimes packed into exploding rockets. The dung was mixed with various poisons and irritants such as croton oil, arsenic, sulphur, mustard, and aconitine to make a chemical weapon known as a 'magic smoke apparition'. They were apparently very effective if they went off in an enclosed space.

Animal fodder

Pigs are very fond of excrement and in rural Asia privies are often built over food troughs so that the pigs get to it when it's as fresh as possible. Sometimes this can cause problems as hungry pigs tend to get overexcited when they see the toilet in use: in 1994 a tourist using a Thai privy spent eight days in hospital after a pig jumped up and bit his backside, though quite whether the pig was impatient for a meal or simply psychotic is not known!

Human dung and urine are both used to feed dogs and reindeer (*see* Cold Weather Crapping, p. 63).

Textile Industry

In the days before soap, urine was often used to clean wool and linen prior to dying. It was also used in the production of some dyes. People who cleaned cloth were known as fullers, and their shops often had a public urinal outside to ensure a regular supply.

This practice survived into the 19th century and British mill owners often paid their workers for their pee (known as 'lant'). In some parts of Manchester a household's urine was stored in a special cask in the street, while in Wales a character popularly known as 'piss Dick' or 'piss Joe' would go door-to-door buying urine at 1d a bucket. Redheads got 1¹/₂d a bucket as their urine was thought to be more potent.

Urine was also used to wash manufactured garments. In 1493 the haberdashers of Paris appealed to the king to prevent fullers from washing bonnets in piss, a habit that the fastidious haberdashers considered neither 'proper or appropriate'.

Other Uses

TOBACCO CURING – tobacco was sometimes cured by hanging it in privies or over vats of urine. In Cuba, cigar makers often soaked the leaves in their urine to soften them prior to rolling.

TANNING – human urine is used to tan leather in many parts of the world and in Mexico human faeces also played a part in the process. In the British army it was customary to soften up a new pair of boots by peeing in them and leaving them to soak overnight.

CHEESE MAKING – in 1802 a Berlin cheese maker was prosecuted for adding young girls' urine to his produce. Urine made the cheeses richer and they were very popular with the locals even after they discovered the nature of the secret ingredient.

CLEANING – urine mixed with bracken ash makes a paste used to polish pewter. Human urine can be used to remove ink stains.

Threepenny Bits

IN emergencies desert tribesmen used to slaughter a camel and drink the fluid in its bladder.

STRICT old-time schoolmasters hardened their canes by soaking them in urine.

HOLY SHIT!

The Old Gods

In ancient times many gods had lavatorial associations. For example in Mexico the goddess Tlazeltectl, goddess of love and carnal pleasure, was also known as the 'The Eater of Ordure'. Her nickname referred to the fact that she was required to listen to the off-colour confessions of sinners who had committed crimes of carnality. Oddly enough the Mexican word for 'gold' translates as 'excrement of the Gods'.

A similar connection can also be seen in Cloacina, Roman goddess of sewers and privies, who is thought to have been a manifestation of Venus, the goddess of love. Another Roman god, Stercutius, was the 'dung god' prayed to by farmers hoping for fertile fields. Crepitus, god of 'convenience' (and, some say, flatulence) was prayed to by those suffering from diarrhoea or constipation.

In Assyria the local version of the goddess Venus is said to have demanded offerings of dung, though whether this was animal, human, or both is not clear. A deity who was offered human excrement was Bel-Phegor a god of the biblical Moabites who was sometimes identified with Beelzebub. Worshippers of Bel-Phegor approached him backwards, bared their backsides and squeezed out an 'offering' (either a turd or a fart) on his altar. It is said that Bel-Phegor ordered that all the human orifices be exposed to him in turn, demanding an offering from each – it must have been an unpleasant job to pass around the collection plate.

Jews

The Bible has some handy hints regarding sanitation. The following passage comes from Deuteronomy, chapter 23 in which God gives some camping advice to the Israelites:

> Thou shalt have a place also without the camp, whither thou shalt go forth abroad: And thou shalt have a paddle upon thy weapon; and it shall be, when thou wilt ease thyself abroad, thou shalt dig therewith, and shalt turn back and cover that which cometh from thee.

Some Jews were very particular about defecation, preferring to go in a cave where the light of day could not reach them. If forced to defecate in the open they would crouch so that their robes hid everything from view – hence the biblical euphemism for defecation, 'hiding your feet'. This practice was not, however, carried on entirely in the name of modesty; it also prevented the pure rays of the sun from being defiled by contact with excrement. Some orthodox Jews were so sensitive about the unclean nature of evacuation that they never pondered on holy matters while crapping and many refused to go on the Sabbath at all.

Crapping was also considered by many Jews to be a dangerous business as they believed that the latrine was the domain of an excrement-eating devil who could force his way into a body during defection. The wife of one Jewish scholar would even go so far as to scare off evil spirits by rattling a brass dish while her husband was relieving himself. Later it was decided that this precaution was insufficient and the wife placed a protective hand over her husband's head while he did his business. Perhaps it's not surprising that *gehenna*, the Jewish name for hell, was also the name of a human dung heap outside Jerusalem.

Hindus

In India the 'Aryan Code of Toilets' (written in around 1500BC) lays down strict rules about defecation. First you had to choose your site carefully. If you were urinating you needed to be at least 10 cubits from the nearest water source, but if you were passing solids the distance was extended to 100 cubits. In the vicinity of a temple these distances were multiplied by four.

Taking a water jar you squatted facing north if it was day, or south if it was night, and placed a cloth or sacred thread over your head. A short mantra was then chanted after which you proceeded to do your business taking care not to look at anything holy like a Brahmin, a fire, or the stars. After defecation you had to use your water pot to wash your genitals once and your anus three times. Your left hand (used for wiping) was then washed ten times and the right hand seven times. You also cleaned your feet. After washing you then rubbed your genitals, anus, hands and feet with earth to remove any lingering smells and had a final sluice with water. After which it was probably time to go again.

The more religious you were, the more strictly you had to follow these rules. The Hindu priestly caste, the Brahmin, are very fastidious. Some Brahmin were so fearful of polluting themselves that the task of bottom-cleaning was delegated to their wives, the job being too important to leave in the hands of servants. Hindus are much less fussy when it comes to the excrement of sacred cows. A rub-over with cow manure or urine is considered purifying and the very devout take it internally. In the past, converts to Hinduism have been required to eat holy cow dung, starting with a pound of dung a day, and slowly diminishing over a six-month period. If someone killed a cow they had to spend a month living in the cattle stables living off cow products, i.e. milk, curds, butter, urine and dung.

At the other end of the hygiene scale are the *bhangi* or 'scavengers' who have the job of emptying latrines. When cleaning privies, bhangis are not allowed to enter the house and can only gain access to the lavatory through a small trapdoor. The cesspit is then scraped clean from the inside and the contents carried out in a basket. Bhangis were looked on with disgust and were not allowed to drink from public wells, enter temples or attend schools. If a high-caste Hindu accidentally touched a bhangi they would then attempt to pass on the defilement by touching a Muslim. If a Brahmin so much as heard the voice of a bhangi while eating he risked pollution and the unfortunate bhangi was liable to receive a nasty punishment involving a red-hot poker.

Human ordure did play a part in some Hindu rituals. A

famous Hindu temple in Mysore used to be visited by childless couples. Pilgrims would pray in the temple then defecate into an open sewer. Water was then drunk from the sewer and a quantity of excrement taken out and formed into a pile on the ground. The couple returned three days later and pulled it apart. If the pile was found to be full of insect life it was taken as a sign that fertility had been restored.

A curious Hindu sect, the Aghozis, are required to eat and drink whatever is given to them, even if it's an old turd. Many carry human excrement around with them and smear it over their bodies. Others threaten to throw it at anyone who won't give them a charitable donation.

Muslims

Muslims consider privies unclean places that must be entered left foot first. When defecating, Muslims must not squat so that they are looking at the sun or the moon, nor may they face Mecca or have their backs to it. A Muslim who buys a home where the toilet faces towards or away from Mecca will often have it repositioned at an angle rather than have to squat on it sideways.

Prayers against Satan are said before evacuation, and a short prayer of thanks is said afterwards. Traditionally the anus is wiped with stones held in the left hand. Wiping is always done with an odd number of stones, as this was what Mohammed used. After wiping, the anus and hands are thoroughly cleaned with water.

Traditionally Muslim men squat to pee as well as defecate for fear that they might accidentally splash themselves with urine. In fact some have suggested that that the Muslim custom of circumcision was adopted in order to prevent drops of urine from touching the foreskin. In the 19th century the English explorer Richard Burton disguised himself as a Muslim and visited Mecca. Any attempt by a Christian to enter the shrine was punishable by death, and on one occasion Richard gave himself away by standing to pee. Luckily only one man saw him and Richard was able to kill him before he gave the game away.

Muslims are very careful to dry themselves after urinating and in the past they used to rub themselves with a stone, or against a wall to rid themselves of moisture. There's a story that a Christian doctor in Constantinople noticed that one particular wall was habitually used for this sort of wiping and secretly covered the stonework with hot pepper. The resulting discomfort caused the Muslims to think they'd caught some sort of venereal disease. The men hurried to the doctor who first suggested amputation as a cure, then sold the appalled Muslims an alternative 'quack' remedy consisting of some expensive unguents and bandages.

Buddhists

It's been said that the droppings of the Lord Buddha glowed in the dark, and for centuries a similar holiness was attributed to those of the Dalai Lama. The droppings of the Dalai Lama were regularly collected, dried and powdered then sold to the faithful or given as gifts to distinguished visitors. His excrement was so valuable that it was sometimes used as currency. It was often packed in dried form into protective amulets worn around the neck. Others used it as a health-giving condiment, sprinkling it on meats at banquets. Still others used it as a medicinal snuff to provoke sneezing.

Christians

Most Christians seem to have been quite matter-of-fact about going to the toilet and there's little in the New Testament about it. Some used faeces as a sign of humility; the beatified Marie Alacoque ate the faeces of diseased people and Antoinette Bouvignon de la Porte mixed dung in her food as a sign of mortification.

According to early Christian scholars, Jesus had perfect digestion and didn't have to defecate, an attribute he shared with the angels of Heaven. Non-defecation was seen as a sign of saintliness and some devout souls attempted to prove their faith by hanging on for as long as possible. Saint Catherine of Sienna is said to have died from constipation after withholding her stools, and a certain Sister Petronella tried to emulate her by not defecating for eight months. (A similar tale is told of a Muslim cleric who was challenged to a fast. Both the cleric and the challenger lasted 40 days before calling a draw. The competition was then changed to see who could go the longest without going to the toilet and the pious cleric won.)

Some saints had miraculous droppings. It's said that a young woman once raided the chamber pot of the 14th century saint, Giovanni Columbini. She smeared the excrement over her facial disfigurement which disappeared completely.

Although Christians knew of the Jewish superstitions regarding defecation they did not abstain from religious thoughts while on the loo. In fact, a St Gregory even went so far as to recommend the privy as a place for religious contemplation. If you did feel the devil creeping up on you in the toilet, the Protestant reformer Martin Luther recommended that you swear at him, and crap and fart in his face. One of Luther's favourite anti-Satan curses was, 'I have shit in the pants, and you can hang them around your neck and wipe your mouth with it'. Luther was said to suffer from severe constipation and probably had more time than most to think up these bon mots.

In a similar vein, Sir John Harington's *The Metamorphosis of Ajax* (1596) tells the story of a holy man who is saying his prayers on the toilet. The devil appears to the man telling him that to speak prayers on the privy is ungodly, whereupon the man retorts that his prayers are going up to heaven while his excrement is going down to hell.

Threepenny Bits

THE Pope used to be carried in the 'Sedes Stercoraria' or 'Fecal Throne'; a portable chair with a potty hole in the seat.

THE Holy Roman Emperor, Charles V, was born in a privy in the Palace of Ghent.

IN the Middle East mosques frequently have a foot-washing area by the door resembling a Western urinal. Signs politely ask tourists not to pee in them.

CARDINAL Wolsey often gave audiences while sitting on his close-stool.

Royal Souvenirs

THEY may not count as near-deities these days but like the Dalai Lama, the toilet products of royals the world over have always been secretly coveted. While most royal souvenir collections are made up of mugs and plates, some are a little more intimate. Rumour has it that when the Royal Yacht Britannia was refitted the old mahogany loo seats were recycled to make presentation cigarette boxes. In a similar vein the loo seat used by Queen Alexandria during a visit to a naval base was removed from its mounting and hung on a wall.

EVEN more bizarrely, it is rumoured that in the past and even today some unscrupulous collectors will do anything, even scout the tracks behind the Royal train, to unearth the ultimate Royal product! One legend has it that a current senior Windsor male left an unflushable 'crowd-pleaser' in the bowl on a visit to a naval base. So impressive was this offering it was decided to remove it for preservation. Apparently it now bobs about in a jar of formaldehyde on the shelf of the naval bar.

OTHER similar tales tell of recovered Royal droppings being variously varnished or bronzed, and mounted on wooden plaques by proud private collectors.

You've got to start somewhere...

the
BATHROOM
book

... and whether you're modernising an old home, or starting from scratch with a new one, "Ideal-Standard" bathroom equipment starts you off in style.

Your own instinctive good taste will tell you that here is true craftsmanship and inspired elegance ... the ideal match between pure beauty and intelligent, modern design.

Start today by sending for the "Ideal-Standard" Bathroom Book. You can browse through it and study the superb design at your leisure. Then start thinking in terms of *your* bathroom. Think "Ideal-Standard".

CUSTOMS AND SUPERSTITIONS

One of the more unusual customs concerning defecation involved the Chaga tribe of East Africa. To convince their womenfolk that they did not need to defecate (and were therefore superior), boys went through a manhood ceremony that involved going out into the jungle and sitting on a thorny bush. The boys' bloodied backsides were then presented as proof that their anuses had been sewn shut. From that day on, all defecation had to be done in secret. Elderly men who found this pantomime a chore went through a second ceremony: their bottoms were smeared with animal blood to show that their anuses had been 'unplugged'.

In Sierra Leone it was the custom to give a person accused of having committed a crime a special potion. If the suspect didn't defecate for 24 hours they were innocent, if they let rip they were found guilty. Presumably this was based on the premise that the guilty would be more nervous than the innocent and more inclined to crap themselves.

The Bambara tribe of West Africa thought that demons lived in excrement and this belief was shared by many others, including the Koreans and Maoris. For this reason toilets have often been regarded as places of ill omen. In Japan loos traditionally face north, a direction of foreboding and bad news.

In North Africa it was believed that evil spirits or *jinnis* lurked in privies and were often to be found sleeping there. If you woke one suddenly they were liable to be bad-tempered and dangerous so it was customary to call out a warning before entering a toilet. The usual cry was '*Rukhsa, ya mubariqin!*' meaning 'With your permission, O blessed ones!' One particularly nasty spirit infesting North African loos was *maezt dar l'oudou*, 'goat of the lavatories'. She could appear anywhere but for some reason was most dangerous in toilets situated near to mosques.

Another female toilet demon known as 'Patni' was found in Bengal. She appeared as an ugly woman with long black hair and club-feet. She was very antisocial and was rumoured to strangle late-night visitors to the bog.

In Australia it was the custom among some Aborigines for a widow to wear human excrement on her head as a sign of mourning. However most Aborigines were careful to bury their excrement in case it fell into the hands of a sorcerer. The belief that your excrement could be used against you in witchcraft was a common one. In fact, among the Indians of Patagonia the latrine of an enemy tribe was considered a great find, enabling you to cause all sorts of mischief. In the Cameroons it was believed that a young woman could absorb someone's soul by smelling their turds.

Similar beliefs were found in the West. In medieval Germany it was thought that if someone left excrement on your property you could get your revenge by pushing fried beans into it, a practice thought to produce agonising pustules on the bottom of the giver. Similarly you could burn the turd with a red-hot poker or pour a mixture of hot wine and pepper over it. Both methods were thought to result in excruciating pain for the turd's former owner. Alternatively you could acquire the thighbone of a man who'd died violently, hollow it out and fill it with your enemy's excrement. If you then sealed the bone with wax and put it in boiling water your victim could be made to crap himself at your command.

Medieval Europeans had a number of magical uses for excrement. An infallible love-potion involved a young woman making a cake by kneading the dough with her backside. A small portion of her poo was included in the mixture and when this dish was fed to a young man he was bound to fall in love with her. In the same way, a German bride could ensure the fidelity of her new husband by peeing in his coffee every morning. Crap could also be used to deter unwanted suitors. If a woman had an unwelcome caller she could put him off by placing a small sample of her faeces in his shoe – which would indeed put most people off. Dung was also believed to be an aphrodisiac; Saxon men used to rub their penises with goat droppings in the belief that it made their lovers randier.

A curious custom of the Middle Ages designed to punish indiscriminate crappers involved confronting someone found defecating near a path or public highway and saying the word 'reverence'. According to tradition, the crapper was then required to take off their hat by biting the brim with their teeth, then flick it backwards over their head. If this tricky task was not accomplished satisfactorily they could be pushed backwards to land in their own droppings.

The Germans seem to have a reputation as prodigious shitters, especially in France. During the First World War a French doctor called Berillon stated that German spies could be detected by the abnormally large volume of turds they produced. According to the doctor this 'excessive' defecation was due to the Germans' unusually long intestinal tract, a feature that made them capable of 'unnatural crimes'.

Good Crap

Crap hasn't always been regarded with ill favour; farmers are well aware of the value of a well-fertilised field. Hence, excrement was often associated with wealth. In many parts of the world it's thought 'lucky' if a bird poops on you. In France it was considered lucky to tread in dung or find some near your door as this meant money was coming your way. Among the Chinese and the Ashanti of Africa to dream of falling in a privy was a sign of great wealth, and in Tangiers anyone who dreamt they'd messed their pants was in for a windfall.

In Europe it was thought that the future of a child could be divined by examining its first defecation. In the Punjab this was taken a little further. At one time it was customary for a grandmother to eat the first defecation of a grandson if it had been born to a long-childless couple or arrived after a string of daughters.

In the past it was thought that a burglar who defecated during a robbery would remain undisturbed. This curious belief is still current in China and every year there are a number of reports of constipated housebreakers being apprehended by the police as they try to drop their guts during a break-in.

The ancient Laplanders maintained that smearing a new boat with the excrement of a virgin would keep it safe from pursuit and out of the clutches of witches.

Pissing

Urine also has its uses. Aedh, a High King of Ireland, believed he'd be blessed if he drank the privy water of a holy cleric, while in Scotland it was considered good luck if the lady of the house showered everyone with her urine on New Year's Day. Midwives did something similar: sprinkling urine on the birthing bed was said to ensure a successful delivery and it was held that a woman's labour pains would be reduced if she drank her husband's urine.

In ancient Egypt it was thought that a pregnant women could predict the sex of her baby by peeing on a wheat seed and a barley seed. If the wheat germinated first it meant she was carrying a boy.

In medieval England it was thought that a woman who peed on nettles would be 'peevish' all day (you would be if you sat on them). Pee was also proof against black magic; if you thought you were under the influence of a witch you could break the spell by peeing through your wedding ring.

The 18th century explorer Mungo Park once stayed overnight in an African village and was woken in the morning by an old woman who threw a bowl of urine in his face. He was told that the piss belonged to a bride due to be married that day and the urine face-wash was a good-luck gift – or perhaps she just didn't like him.

The Hottentots of South Africa had many ceremonial uses for urine as illustrated by this letter from *The Gentleman's Magazine*, February 1731. The author is quoting from *An Account of the Cape of Good Hope* by Kolben:

> To prove this he quotes the custom of the Hottentots initiating a youth into manhood, which is in this manner. First, 'They roundly bedaub him with fat and food, after which the oldest man amongst them pisses with great vigour all over him, which the youth received with an eager care; and making furrows with his long nails in the fat upon his body, rubs and mixes the piss with the fat.' When the old fellow has dribbled upon him to the last drop he felicitates him upon the honour that is done him and crowns him with many benedictions, which he utters aloud. Then is the young fellow proclaimed a man.
>
> The same kind of honour is made part of the marriage ceremony, and the priest pisses on the

bridegroom and the bride alternately till his whole stock of urine is exhausted and then wishes them joy… This ceremony of pissing is again performed at their funerals. Two old fellows, friends or relatives of the deceased piss each upon all the company, which is received with the greatest eagerness and veneration.

Christmas Crappers

IN the fiercely independent Catalan region of Spain there is a mountain of scatological obsession in the local folklore. It comes clearly to the fore during the Christmas festivities when most Catalans build and display nativity scenes. In addition to the figures in the nativity that most of us would recognise – Joseph, Mary and the odd donkey – the Catalans have the caganer: usually a man, but occasionally a woman, happily taking a crap at the birth scene of the King of Kings. It is the most popular figure in the nativity and local craftsman compete each year to create new ever more interesting representations of their beloved caganer.

Threepenny Bits

AN old Scottish law states that if anyone knocks on your door asking to use the toilet you must let them in.

AFTER each of her divorces Joan Craword changed all the loo seats in her house.

ROMAN women drank turpentine to make their urine smell like roses.

IN Siberia a host used to offer his guest a drink containing the urine of his wife or daughter.

ETHELRED the Unready peed in the font during his baptism; this was taken as a bad omen.

IN medieval Naples it was customary for a bankrupt to bare his bottom in front of the Palace of Justice and shout three times, 'Let all my creditors come forward to collect!'

203

RUDE TOILET
BEHAVIOUR

**WARNING! MOST PEOPLE WILL FIND SOMETHING TO
OFFEND THEM IN THIS CHAPTER.**

A great deal has been written on the connection
between sexuality and defecation and most of it is very
boring. Freud suggested that infants went through a
number of stages in sexual development, the first
being oral, and the second a 'sadistic' anal stage. Freud
called it sadistic because the act involves expulsion
and destruction. It also involves control and manipula-
tion, as a child can decide to give or withhold faeces at
will. According to Freud, those that withhold grow up
to be obstinate 'anal retentives', obsessed with order-
liness and reluctant to buy a round of drinks.

The whole subject becomes very complicated if you
delve too deeply; suffice it to say that some people are
turned on by the 'forbidden' and find toilets and everything to do with them quite exciting. Certain phrases in
Mozart's private correspondence suggest that he had

an interest in the scatological, and that brothels are sometimes equipped with glass floors so that patrons can watch girls relieving themselves from below.

Defecation is itself a pleasurable business. Dr Johnson once commented that a 'solid movement of the bowl' was better than intercourse (sexual arousal through defecation being known as 'defecolangnia'). Since nature wants us to defecate regularly it has equipped the anus with numerous nerve endings that make passing a stool a pleasant experience. However this has also resulted in some people regarding the anus as an extra erogenous zone. Every emergency room in the world can report stories concerning the objects that have been used to stimulate this area and become stuck, ranging from the banal (bananas, broom handles, candles etc.), to the bizarre (turnips, artillery shells and frozen pigs' tails).

Voyeurs

Some people enjoy watching people going to the toilet. In the erotic Victorian journal *My Secret Life*, the author, 'Walter', recounts how he finds a convenient knot-hole in the wall of a ladies' toilet at a rural Swiss railway station. He settles in and spends an entire weekend watching female passengers squatting on the privy. Although he admits to not having enjoyed himself very much, he found it hard to tear himself away none the less.

It seems public loos are still a favourite haunt of voyeurs. In 1991 a Connecticut man turned himself in to rangers at a state park admitting he'd been crawling under outhouses in order to look at women using the lavatory. Something similar happened in a Californian state park in 1987 – here a man was found wrapped in plastic, sitting waist-high in the cesspit under the ladies' latrine. Others have used a more high-tech approach. In 1996 a man was arrested for installing secret 'toilet cams' in a number of US ladies' restrooms. Indeed, if their claims are to be believed, there are a number of Internet sites that promise a candid inside view of public toilets via a webcam.

Cottaging

The connection between the male homosexual community and toilets is well known and every year large numbers of gay men are arrested for importuning in public lavatories. This number occasionally includes a celebrity. The most famous recent case involved George Michael who was fined $810 for committing a 'lewd act' in a Los Angeles lavatory. The actor Sir John Gielgud and 1960s heart-throb Peter Wyngarde are others who have been caught out.

Cruising public toilets is sometimes known as 'cottaging', a phrase derived from Victorian times when public toilets, especially those in parks, were known as 'cottages'. A well-known cottaging technique is to walk in carrying a large flat-bottomed paper bag. Once a like-minded individual has been contacted the two retire to a cubicle together and enjoy themselves. One gentleman sits on the toilet while the other stands with his feet in the bag. This means that any park-keeper, policeman or security guard looking under the cubicle door will not see anything suspicious.

Public toilets frequented by gay men are often equipped with 'glory holes' bored through the partitions between cubicles. Glory holes are used to observe the activity in the next cubicle and, if they are wide enough, can ultimately be used as access ports for various parts of the male anatomy.

The Mile-High Club

Sex on passenger aircraft is sometimes done in the seating area but more commonly in the toilets. Although it's usually passengers who indulge in this activity it is not unknown for crew members to do the same. At least one pilot has lost his job after having toilet sex with a flight attendant. Those attendants who have witnessed 'the mile-high club' in action say that the most common arrangement is for the man to sit on the toilet seat while the woman straddles him. For those wanting more visual tips, an act of aeroplane toilet sex appears in the film *Emmanuelle*. Some people find the practice quite addictive, and one female serial mile-high shagger has confessed to loo encounters on 10 different flights.

In a famous incident in 1974 Princess Elizabeth of Toro, a Ugandan diplomat, was caught having sex in the toilets in the airport in Paris. She claimed she was merely discussing 'Ugandan affairs' with a colleague and this phrase was subsequently adopted as a euphemism for sex, particularly by the magazine *Private Eye*.

Toilet Slaves

An unusual breed of fetishists, known as 'toilet slaves', are people who enjoy the sensation of being defecated and urinated on, or who crave the humiliation, or both. Some slaves serve one master or mistress while others enjoy being a shared resource at bondage parties. At such an event the toilet slave will usually be chained up in the bathroom where they might simply lick the toilet clean after use, act as a human bidet, or in extreme cases, a complete sewage disposal system. There are a number of invalid commodes and portable toilets on the market that can be adapted for the use of toilet slaves, the waste bucket being removed to allow the slave to position their face under the seat while lying on the floor.

Coprophagy

The act of eating faeces is called coprophagy. Some toilet slaves do not eat faeces but will hold it in the oral cavity before spitting it out, an activity known as 'mouthing'. To train a slave to eat turds, a master or mistress will sometimes insert corned beef or chocolate mousse up their rectum to simulate faeces.

Not all copropaghes are fetishists. Among the Eskimos it was common for mothers to lick their babies clean after they'd soiled themselves, and in the early Christian church ordure was sometimes eaten by the devout as a sign of humility. Curiously there's a reference to eating excrement in the Old Testament: 'and thou shall eat it as barley cakes and thou shalt bake it with dung that cometh out of man in their sight' (Ezekiel 4:12).

Pope Alexander IV used to tell a cautionary tale about a woman who was molested by a priest. To get her own back she baked the priest a pie containing a number of large turds. The priest was so impressed by the gift he decided to give it to his bishop, who was not so impressed when he took a bite.

Some people enjoy eating excrement. In America one man was so keen to get a supply he used to sabotage the water supply in public toilets so that they were impossible to flush. He'd then nip in with a bag and collect what was left in the bowls. An American sex offender known as the Peanut Butter Kid used to smear his own excrement on his victim's genitals and lick it off.

Excrement, human and animal, is often eaten in cases of extreme starvation. Faeces is surprisingly nutritious and contains a significant number of calories, vitamins, calcium, iron and some protein. Thanks to inefficient digestion approximately 25 per cent of the protein in rice is not digested, the figure being 26 per cent for potatoes and 40 per cent for cornmeal.

Faeces is also a source of vitamin B12. The bacteria in the colon make a large amount of B12 but unfortunately the colon is not able to absorb it. Vegans often suffer from a B12 deficiency and in the 1950s a British doctor tried feeding vegans water extracted from human faeces. In this case the B12 was absorbed in the small bowel and the deficiency was cured.

The nutritional value of excrement has long been recognised in the farming industry, in the USA cattle often being fed fermented chicken manure as a nitrogen supplement. The relatively high protein contents of cat droppings makes them a choice snack for less fastidious dogs, and 25 per cent of the diet of rats and mice consists of their own recycled droppings. Many animals eat faeces (their own and others) including rabbits, lemurs and gorillas, though in many coprophagy is only seen in the young. Some animals are able to utilise their waste without it actually leaving the body, research suggesting that a hibernating bear is able to extract protein from recycled excretion products. This enables a bear to survive the winter months with only a minimal loss of muscle.

As to the taste of faeces, accounts differ: one source claims that it tastes 'charred' but apart from that very similar to the original food; another describes it as tasting of 'rotten Hungarian peppers in a soft cream'; another simply describes it as strong and 'sweetish'. Most people who've tried it agree that it smells worse than it tastes. One eccentric European prince got round the problem of flavour in an ingenious way; he regularly paid his mistress to defecate in his mouth but insisted she live on a diet of marzipan.

It should be said that faeces is essentially decaying bacterial sludge. Eating excrement, your own or other people's, is a deeply unsanitary occupation that is not recommended.

Threepenny Bits

IN 1996 a distinguished but drunken economist was denied any more alcoholic beverages on a flight to New York. To show his displeasure he defecated on the stewardess's serving cart and wiped his bum with the first-class table linen.

RICHARD the Lionheart once threw the banner of the Archduke of Austria down a privy hole. This started a feud that eventually led to Richard's imprisonment.

PEOPLE suffering from 'encopresis' continually crap in 'inappropriate' places.

IN 18th century Paris a gang of young aristocrats roamed the streets making poor people lick their back-sides. They called themselves 'the Brotherhood of Kissed Asses'.

LORD Byron was thrown out of a Bond Street hotel for crapping (some say peeing) in the hall outside his room. He tried to blame the mess on his dog.

ACCORDING to a recent Internet survey, 53 per cent of people pee in the shower.

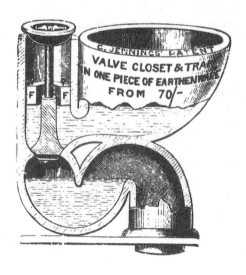

DEATH ON THE LOO

It is very common for people to die on the toilet, the most usual cause being heart failure while straining to pass a stool. When we sit on the loo and attempt to 'lay a cable' we are performing a series of actions known as the Valsalver Manoeuvre. Straining involves contraction of the abdomen and thorax, which tends to reduce the blood flow to the heart. This in itself can cause a stroke, however there's also the risk that you might rupture an 'aneurysm', a weak spot in the wall of a blood vessel. Releasing the tension is just as dangerous: a pulse of blood then rushes to the brain that might carry a fatal blood clot. And as if all this wasn't enough there's also the chance that straining might rupture your spleen.

You shouldn't be unduly alarmed however: according to a survey conducted in Japan in 1989, the toilet is one of the safest rooms in the house. In a sample of household deaths, fatal symptoms first appeared in the toilet in only 8 per cent of cases (as compared with 31 per cent in the bedroom and 17 per cent in the bath). Oddly enough many Japanese people who croak in the loo die of shock. Central heating is rare in Japan and elderly people have been known to collapse with cerebral apoplexy after leaving a nice warm living-room to enter a freezing lavatory.

The most famous toilet death of recent times was Elvis Presley's. Accounts differ but Elvis is said to have been found face down on his toilet floor with his green pyjamas round his ankles. Elvis had numerous botty problems including bleeding piles, a twisted colon and constipation. The cause of death was put down as heart failure, and while it is not known whether or not Elvis was straining, at his autopsy his colon weighed 42 lbs (roughly the size of five bouncing babies).

It was perhaps fitting that the 'King of rock 'n' roll' died on the lavatory. Throughout history numerous other kings have gone the same way.

Royal Deaths

• The biblical king of Moab, Elgon (who lived in the city of Shittim), was murdered in his privy.

• David is said to have slain King Saul during a visit to the toilet.

• In AD79 the Emperor Vespasian 'felt the approach of death' while sitting on his chamber pot.

• In 222 the Roman Emperor Heliogabalus, a notorious voluptuary and homosexual, was stabbed to death in his privy and his body thrown down a sewer.

• The Saxon King Edmund Ironside (son of Ethelred the Unready) ruled briefly before being murdered by a man hiding in the royal privy pit. While Edmund was doing 'number twos' an assassin (acting in the name of Edmunds's rival, King Canute) stabbed him twice up the backside with a spear. Canute was so horrified at this sneaky act carried out in his name he had the murderer beheaded.

• In 1183 (some sources say 1184) the floor of the Great Hall of Erfurt Castle gave way during a banquet held by the Emperor Ferdinand. The hall was built over a cesspit and eight princes and numerous knights drowned in the pool of excrement.

• James I of Scotland was murdered in a privy pit in 1437. The pit was connected to the chimney in his room and he had been hiding there to escape a band of assassins.

• In 1760 King George II of England is said to have collapsed on the toilet after letting rip a colossal fart. He fell off the seat and hit his head on some furniture.

• Some say that Catherine the Great of Russia died having sex with a horse. However the constipated empress really died straining on the lavatory in 1796. She was discovered lying on the floor by her commode foaming at the mouth. She'd suffered a stroke and died a few hours later.

• In 1957 King Harkon VII of Norway slipped on some soap in the royal bathroom and fatally fractured his skull on the taps.

• *The one that got away*: Robert the Bruce, King of Scotland (1274–1329), was a man of regular habits and, on paying his morning visit to the privy, discovered three assassins waiting for him. Luckily Bruce was armed and managed to slaughter his attackers after some nifty swordplay.

Not-So-Royal Deaths

• A story from the *Chronicle of London* tells of a 13th-century Jew in Tewkesbury who happened to fall into a public latrine on a Saturday. Since it was the Jewish day of rest the man refused to let anyone pull him out and he stayed in the cesspit till Sunday morning. The Earl of Gloucester (some say the Bishop of Gloucester) heard about the incident and decreed that no one should pull him out on the Christian day of rest. By the time Monday arrived the man was dead.

• In an English prison in 1843, a group of 21 female prisoners were confined in a rarely used room while their cells were inspected. The floor gave way and 20 of the women fell into an ancient cesspit below. Five drowned before they could be rescued.

• In 1856 a man in the English town of Lewes entered a public latrine in the High Street unaware that the floorboards had been removed during maintenance. He fell into the cesspit and was asphyxiated by the fumes.

• According to legend, in 1934 the Hollywood actress Lupe Velez ('the Mexican spitfire') overdosed on some sleeping pills. Feeling sick she ran to the toilet where she slipped, ended up face first in the toilet bowl, and drowned.

• In 1962 an Englishman killed his wife then stuck his head in the toilet bowl. He then flushed until he'd drowned himself.

• Evelyn Waugh died in 1966 of a coronary thrombosis while perched on the downstairs lavatory of his home.

• In 1969 Judy Garland was found slumped, fully dressed, on the toilet of a London hotel. She had succumbed to an accidental overdose of prescription pills.

• Convicted murderer Michael Godwin died on the toilet in 1989. The toilet of his South Carolina cell was made of stainless steel and he was sitting on it while trying to repair a portable TV. Biting through a live wire he made a circuit and electrocuted himself.

• At a double wedding celebration of two Jordanian brothers in 1990, the dance floor gave way, dropping the guests into a cesspit below. Thirteen people drowned including both brides.

• In 1993 a Korean immigrant living in Chicago killed himself trying to spend a penny. The man relieved himself on some railway tracks, hit the live rail, and was electrocuted.

• In 1994 a German man dropped his wallet down an outhouse cesspit. Attempting to retrieve it he toppled into the sewage and drowned.

• In 1995 a man was killed on the Isle of Wight when his metal lavatory made contact with a faulty electric cable.

• A similar tale is told of murderer Laurence Baker who was electrocuted in 1997. Laurence was fried wearing a pair of faulty home-made earphones while sitting on a metal prison toilet in Pittsburgh.

• A Bavarian man was apparently electrocuted on the loo while using a home-made 'marital aid' cobbled together out of an electric potato masher. The masher was attached to the mains and when the man pulled on the toilet chain he created a circuit that killed him.

• A report from Miami tells of a Mexican construction worker who was killed by a falling toilet. The toilet, a portable latrine, had blown off the fourth floor of a neighbouring construction project.

• *The one that got away*: a woman watching a rodeo in North Dakota was so disturbed by the injuries being inflicted on a bull rider she went to the ladies' to recover. In the meantime a bull managed to jump the fences, charged down a corridor and burst through the door of the woman's toilet cubicle. The woman was pinned to the wall and suffered an injured shoulder and arm before being rescued.

TOILETS, HUMOUR AND THE ARTS

The Arts

Not surprisingly, toilets and excrement only play a limited role in the art world, however there are examples to be found. Belgian artist Jacques Lizene is one of these, painting, as he does, using his own excrement. Brown is a rather limiting colour by itself so after much trial and error Jacques has developed some dietary techniques that allow him to choose the colour of his excrement. Oddly enough most of Jacques's 'crap' paintings are pictures of brickwork. More recently young Brit artist Chris Ofili won the prestigious Turner Prize for, among other things, a series of canvases that incorporated dollops of elephant dung in to the composition.

A number of companies now sell decorated toilet seats. Some are hand-painted, while others are made of transparent plastic and enclose objects such as lengths of barbed wire, flowers, and seashells. In Texas there is even a Toilet Seat Art Museum, housing hand-decorated seats created by the artist Barney Smith.

The best known example of toilet-based 'installation art' is Duchamp's 'Fountain'. Marcel Duchamp (1887-1968) was a French artist who, under the pseudonym of Mr Mutt, entered a urinal (the 'Fountain') into an exhibition organised by the New York Society of Independent Artists in 1917. The urinal was unusual in that it was signed and hung upside down but the Society didn't consider it an original artistic creation and the work was rejected. Duchamp defended the urinal with these words, 'Whether Mr Mutt with his own hands made the fountain or not has no importance. He chose. He took an ordinary article of life, placed it so that its useful significance disappeared under a new title and point of view ... [creating] a new thought for that object.'

There are few performance artists who deal with defecation, an exception being the US artist Alexander Brener. Apart from having sex with his wife in public, stapling things to his buttocks, and masturbating in a public swimming pool, Mr Brener once went into a museum and defecated in front of a Van Gogh. It's not certain whether this was a statement or he was simply desperate to go.

The farting Frenchman Joseph Pujol (1857-1945) deserves a mention here, although his toilet connection is a little more tenuous. Joseph achieved fame as *Le Petomane* (The Fart-Maniac) after he discovered he could suck air into his rectum and expel it at will. This talent enabled him to make a variety of humorous sound effects and to perform tricks with it such as blowing out candles and smoking cigarettes. For many years he was one of France's highest-paid performers.

Literature

The world of literature is a richer source of toilet-related art:

JONATHAN SWIFT
The Anglo-Irish satirist, poet and clergyman Jonathan Swift, most famous for *Gulliver's Travels* (1726), had more than a passing interest in the lavatory and once published a treatise on excrement, entitled *Human Ordure*, under the pseudonym Dr Shit.

EVELYN WAUGH
Evelyn Waugh's *Sword of Honour* trilogy opens with a story called 'Men at Arms' which tells of a bizarre duel over a field latrine known as the 'thunder box'. The story is set in an Army training camp during the Second World War where Apthorpe, an eccentric

corporal is the proud owner of the thunder box, an item he acquired from a colonial high court judge. Unfortunately for Apthorpe the commode is coveted by his barmy superior, Brigadier Ritchie-Hook who steals it and declares it 'out of bounds to all ranks below brigadier'. The two men take turns stealing the box from each other until the brigadier decides to end the game once and for all; he booby-traps the commode and poor Apthorpe is blown to bits.

CHARLES BUKOWSKI
The autobiographical stories of American author Charles Bukowski detail his low-life existence in Los Angeles. Suffering a mild bowel fixation Bukowski confesses that he fears constipation more than cancer: 'If I miss one day without shitting, I can't go anywhere, do anything.' One of his stories involves a blocked toilet in his apartment. The landlord is away on holiday and unwilling, or unable, to fix it himself Bukowski resorts to fishing turds out of the bowl, putting them in brown paper bags and leaving them round the neighbourhood.

ANTHONY BURGESS
Anthony Burgess's character Enderby who appears in several of his novels, including *The Clockwork Testament* and *Enderby's Dark Lady*, was a rather eccentric writer and poet who composed his verse on the toilet.

James Joyce

James Joyce's *Ulysses* (first published in 1922) contains a fair amount of farting and a graphic, though restrained, description of a bowel movement (for many people this small glimpse into the toilet habits of the novel's main character was a glimpse too much; the book was banned in Britain and America):

> He kicked open the crazy door of the jakes. Leaving the door ajar, amid the stench of mouldy limewash and stale cobwebs he undid his braces. The king was in his counting house. Asquat the cuckstool he folded out his paper turning its pages over on his bare knees. Quietly he read, restraining himself, the first column and, yielding but resisting, began the second. Midway, his last resistance yielding, he allowed his bowels to ease themselves quietly as he read, reading still patiently, that slight constipation of yesterday quite gone. Hope it's not too big to bring on the piles again. No, just right. He read on seated calmly above his own rising smell.

Our hero's reading matter in this instance is a prize-winning short story, and unimpressed with it, he then uses it to wipe his arse.

François Rabelais

Sixteenth century French monk and satirist, François Rabelais, created a character called Gargantua who devoted himself to a study of bottom-wiping materials. These items included: a ladies' neckerchief, a page's cap (garnished with a feather), his mother's gloves, sheets, a tablecloth, cushions, sage, fennel, marjoram, roses, beets, mangy dogs, wool, straw, flax, a falconer's lure, a hen, a cock, a pullet, a pigeon and a hare. 'Shaggie hats' were popular, but cats were a no-no as they scratched too much. His favourite bum-wiping material is revealed in the following, 'I say and maintain, that of all the torcheculs, arsewisps, bumfodders, tail-napkins, bunghole cleansers and wipe-breeches, there is none in the world comparable to the neck of a goose.' Oddly enough paper is very low on his list, Gargantua declaring that, 'Who his foule taile with paper wipes, Shall at his ballocks leave some chips.' Gargantua also composed a poem regarding those who do not wipe:

Shittard
Squirtard
Crackard
Turduous:
Thy bung
Hath flung
Some dung
On us:
Filthard
Cackard
Stinkard,

St Antoine's fire
seize on thy toane
If thy
Dirty
Dounby
Thou do not wipe
ere thou be gone.

Victorian Toilet Rhymes

'Oh Cloacina, goddess of this place, look on thy servant with a smiling face. Soft and cohesive let my offering flow not rudely swift, or obstinately slow.'

'To Kings and Queens we bend the knee, but Queens themselves are forced to stoop to thee.'

Toilets at the Movies

The cinema is a positive fountain of 'toilet moments' both dramatic and humorous. One of the most bizarre occurs in the 1994 film *Clerks*, in which although you don't actually see any of the action, the main character's girlfriend manages to accidentally have sex with a dead pensioner she finds slumped in a latrine.

A Top Ten of Cinematic Toilet Scenes

Carry on Screaming (1966) in which a Victorian toilet attendant, Dan Dann 'the gardening man' (Charles Hawtrey), is drowned in his own toilet by the reanimated corpse of a sub-human monster.

2001: A Space Odyssey (1968) in which a confused passenger on a spaceship tries to interpret the directions on a zero gravity toilet.

The Naked Gun (1988) in which Frank Drebin (Leslie Nielsen) accidentally takes a microphone into the gents with him and broadcasts sounds of noisy and copious urination over a PA system.

Lethal Weapon II (1989) in which Danny Glover sits on the toilet in his bathroom only to discover it's been booby-trapped, and as soon as he gets off it will explode. Mel Gibson saves the day by pulling Glover off the loo and into the safety of the bathtub.

Jurassic Park (1993) in which a rogue tyrannosaur chomps a man who is sitting on a chemical toilet.

Dumb and Dumber (1994) in which Jim Carrey secretly doses Jeff Daniels with laxative. In a noisy and prolonged crapping session Jeff is forced to pollute his girlfriend's broken toilet.

Pulp Fiction (1994) in which John Travolta's character is a keen toilet reader who is eventually machine-gunned to death in the bathroom.

Species (1995) in which a girl has her spine torn out while sitting on a toilet in a night-club.

Trainspotting (1996) in which Ewan McGregor slips into a filthy toilet and swims, in a very surreal sequence, to the bottom of the bowl to retrieve some discarded pills.

Austin Powers (1997) in which an assassin attempts to strangle Austin in the cubicle of a public toilet. Tom Arnold, who is sitting in the next cubicle, thinks Austin is simply struggling to release a huge turd and chips in with numerous encouraging comments.

Toilet Humour

That institution of British toilet humour *Viz* has created a number of toilet-based cartoon characters. Among them are: The Bottom Inspector with his catchphrase, 'Have you wiped properly?'; Shitty Dick, who battles against a compulsion to defecate in front of members of the clergy; Dr Poo, a Tom Baker look-a-like searching the galaxy for an empty lavatory; Dr Poolittle, a constipated Rex Harrison; and Rat Boy, a juvenile delinquent constantly relieving himself in other people's property.

Graffiti

The scientific name for toilet graffiti is 'coprography'. According to a recent British Rail survey 77 per cent of men's toilet cubicles were defaced, as against 79 per cent of the ladies' (the difference probably being attributable to the extra time spent in the latter).

The earliest recorded toilet graffiti are from Greek and Roman times (*see* History of the Toilet, Part One, p. 1), Here are some of the better-known modern examples of the art form:

Men are like public toilets, they're either vacant, engaged, or full of shit.

Don't look up here for a joke, you've got one in your hand.

I thought Wanking was a town in China, till I went blind.

Don't throw your fag ends in the loo, it makes them impossible to light.

Antisocial diseases are a sore point.

If you can aim this high you should join the fire-brigade.

Diarrhoea waits for no man.

And the classic:

Here I sit broken hearted, paid a penny and only farted.

Practical Jokes

Perhaps the best-known toilet joke is to put cling-film over the toilet seat. Another one was a favourite of independent filmmaker, Russ Meyer: many of Russ's movies were filmed in the Californian desert and when the opportunity arose Russ would follow a cast or crew-member when they walked into the wilds to take a dump. He would carefully position himself behind the squatting victim then gently push a long-handled spade underneath their exposed backside. Once the faeces had dropped on to the shovel Russ would quickly withdraw it and make himself scarce. The victim would then wipe, stand up, and try to figure out where on earth their turd had vanished to. For those wanting a visual reference this joke was immortalised in celluloid in Russ's 1979 film, *Beneath the Valley of the Ultra Vixens*.

Threepenny Bits

A toilet-based musical called *Flush* was launched in 1996. The action takes place in the unisex restroom of a hall that is simultaneously hosting a funeral and a wedding.

THE rock group Slade often recorded their drum tracks and hand claps in the toilet of their recording studio. They liked the hard 'edge' of the acoustics.

THE Roman writer Pliny said that peeing where a dog had peed previously would lead to a numbness of the loins.

MOST American toilets apparently flush in 'E flat'.

THE first flushing toilet to be heard in the cinema was in the 1959 film *Psycho*.

A Japanese TV character called 'Ugo Ugo Ruga' or 'Dr Stinky' is a talking turd with big eyebrows.

LEGENDARY rock star Ozzy Osbourne once had chamber pots made featuring his own (made up) coat of arms. After the female members of his household complained about his poor peeing-aim he also had a private urinal installed in the family bathroom.

LEONARDO da Vinci once designed a castle that had toilets with automatic doors and flushing channels hidden inside the walls.

WORDS AND PHRASES

Euphemisms

Since going to the toilet is often regarded as a sensitive matter a number of euphemisms have been coined to describe the act. In the days when even grand houses had outside toilets, ladies would go into the garden to 'pluck a rose' or 'plant a sweet pea', and the introduction of paying public toilets led to people 'spending a penny'. Other delicate phrases that have sprung include to: 'visit the house of necessity'; 'visit Mrs Jones'; 'go to the House of Commons/Lords'; 'off to India'; 'powder one's nose'; 'see a man about a dog'; 'do one's business'; 'do the necessary'; 'shake the dew off the Lilly'; 'freshen up'; 'visit the little boys'/girls' room'; 'go to the throne room'. A somewhat less delicate old-time expression was 'to go where all the big nobs hang out'.

A curious phrase found in a number of countries is 'I must go to where even the Queen goes alone', the word 'Queen' being substituted for the title of the local ruler. A variation on this is the German phrase, *Der Ort, wo auch der Kaiser zu Fuß hingeht*, meaning, 'I must go where even the Kaiser goes on foot', presumably because the Kaiser went everywhere else on horseback.

Euphemisms of all Nations

To the ancient Egyptians the toilet was the 'house of morning', while in Israel the lavatory was known, sarcastically we presume, as the 'house of honour'. Today visitors to the loo in Arabic countries are said to be 'filling the hole'. In South Africa people visit the 'small house' (*Kleinhuisie*) while Ugandan men going to pee are said to be going for a 'short call'. In Cuba those who wish to excuse themselves say 'I have to write a letter' (*Tengo que escribir una carta*). In France you say you're going to *la chambre sent* (the 'smelly room'), the 'little corner' (*le petit coin*), or 'number 100', *au numéro 100* (*see* Public Toilets, p. 101). In Russia you might 'go to the field' (*meydana gitmek*), or 'make a phone call'. (This latter expression was both a euphemism and a joke regarding the state of the Soviet phone network – no one would ever think you were really making a call because the phones

238

never worked.) The English term 'WC' has taken root in a number of countries (*see* Crappers of All Nations, p. 159): the Finns, for example, referring to the toilet as a vessa or veesee.

The Chinese, being a discreet people, have developed a number of modest expressions. Urinating is a 'small convenience', while defecation is a 'big convenience'. A visit to the toilet may be described as 'going to a remarkable meeting of philosophers and friends' or 'going to the Hall of Brotherhood' both of which reflect the fact that most Chinese use communal toilets (*see* Crappers of All Nations, p. 159). People departing to the loo might wish that 'heaven grant happiness'. An old Chinese expression for a toilet stop is to 'let go of your hands': in ancient China prisoners who were being marched round the country had their hands tied. If they wished to go to the toilet they'd have to ask a guard to release them.

Vulgar Slang

Not surprisingly there are many crude terms for defecation and everything associated with it. In the following we take great pleasure in providing you with a selection. For example, if you were walking down the street the first sign of trouble might be if you…

backfired / broke company/ blew off

…and let rip an…

*air biscuit / anal announcement / afterburner /
backwards burp / botty burp / bowel bugle /
bowel howl / blanket ripper / bronx cheer*

…you might then discover you had…

*one on the slipway / the horse's head / the turtle's
head / the pup's head*

…and were…

*chewing on a brick / doing a cowboy walk /
smuggling a brownie / in Itchypoo Park.*

In extreme cases you might even be…

touching cloth / touching socks.

In this instance you would hurry to the nearest…

*bog / bunko booth / cludgie / cottage / crapper /
dunny / eric / gurgler / jane / john / khazi / nettie /
parlour / slash palace / throne / thunder box /
thunder mug / trap / turdis.*

WORDS AND PHRASES

Once in the toilet you would sit your…

bahookie / dock / duff / hummer / jacksie / scooter

…on the seat, positioning your…

*balloon knot / barking spider / blurter / brass eye /
brown bullet hole / brown eye / chocolate eye /
chocolate starfish / cornhole / corybungo / dark star /
freckle / glory hole / Japanese flag / keister / mud
hole / mudeye / nether eye / poot flute / quoit / rusty
sheriff's badge / tea-towel holder / wazoo / winking
walnut*

…over the bowl, then wait for something to emerge
from your…

*backpassage / bomb bay / Bourneville boulevard /
Cadbury alley / chutney locker / date locker / dirtbox /
dung funnel / exhaust pipe / fudge tunnel / Hershey
highway / loon pipe / Marmite motorway / muck
spreader / nether throat / poop chute.*

If successful you would soon…

*build a log cabin / have a burial at sea / bury a
Quaker / crimp off a length / curl one off / drop a
pebble / drop the kids off at the pool /*

*drop the shopping / drown the chocolate slugs /
drown a mole / dump / grow a tail / heave a Havana /
lay a cable / lay and display / papper / park the
fudge / park your breakfast / pinch a loaf / rake the
cage out / ride the porcelain bus / see a friend to the
coast / send a sausage to the seaside / sing sweet
violets / sink a U-boat / sink the Bismark/ strangle a
darkie / turn your bike around / unload*

…the result of your efforts being…

*an Admiral Browning / a belly flopper / a Bovril
bullet / a bobber / a brown trout / a bum cigar /
a chocolate iceberg / a chocolate shark / a copper
bolt / a crowd pleaser / a curler / a depth charge /
a floater / a groaner / a jobby / a log / a lurker /
a tail ender / a U-blocker / a tree log / a twinkie /
a whoopsy/ a plop / a HOP ('hang over poo')*

…or some…

*arse feta / Blackpool rock / cack / clarts / gick /
grogan / grunties / kak / mud.*

That is, unless you were suffering from…

*Gippy tummy / Franco's revenge / Montezuma's
revenge / Delhi belly / the squirts / the squits / the trots*

…and were doing the…

Aztec two-step / sour apple quickstep / Tijuana cha-cha / Turkish two-step / La Turista

…in which case you might…

blow mud / pebble dash / go crop-spraying / spend tuppence in ha'pennies and farthings

…and produce…

arse piss / bum gravy / mung / rusty water

…in which case you might be left with a…

red ring / ring sting / ringburner

…and you might find that your underwear had developed a…

russet gusset / skid mark / Marmite stripe.

After finishing you'd be careful to clean yourself properly otherwise your backside might be graced by…

bum conkers / bum crumbs / bumtags / chuff nuts /

*clinkers / dags / dangleberries / dillberries / fartle-
berries / hairy toffee / kling-ons / a langball / mince
medallions / a mustang / tagnuts / toffee strings /
willnots / winnets.*

Alternatively, you might just be emptying your bladder in which case you'd…

*aim Archie at the Armitage / wring the rattlesnake /
point Percy at the porcelain / shake the snake /
splash your boots / strain your greens / siphon the
python / waz.*

Rhyming Slang

Aris – Aristotle – bottle – bottle and glass – ARSE
Big hit – SHIT
Chalfonts – Chalfont St Giles – PILES
Council gritter – SHITTER
Ertha Kitts – SHITS
Emmas – Emma Freuds – HAEMORRHOIDS
Engleburt – Engleburt Humperdinck – STINK
Farmers – Farmer Giles – PILES
Florins – a.k.a. two-bob-bits – SHITS
Gary Glitter – SHITTER
Gypsies – gypsy's kiss – PISS
Hit and miss – PISS
Jimmy Britts – SHITS

Khyber Pass – ARSE
Michaels – Michael Miles – PILES
My word – TURD
Nauticals – nautical miles – PILES
Nobbies – Nobbie Stiles – PILES
Plymouth Argyles – PILES
Pony – pony and trap – CRAP
Richard – Richard III – TURD
Rockfords – Rockford Files – PILES
Ronson – Ronson lighter – SHITER
Thora Hird – TURD
Threepenny bits – SHITS
Toms – Tom Tits – SHITS
Trays – tray bits – SHITS
Whirling pits – SHITS

School and University Slang

Over the years, a number of slang expressions for toilets have developed in British public schools. In Harrow (among others) they are known as 'the rears'. Rugby has adopted the Classical Greek term, *Topos* ('a place'). Lancing and others use the term 'the groves' (presumably because in the old days much crapping was done in the woods), while Marlborough students simply call them, 'the woods'. Oundle uses the term 'dykes' which is also Australian slang for the same place, while North Foreland Lodge calls them 'the Bogies', Felstead, 'the shankies' and Worth, 'the yard'.

At Balliol College, Oxford, students pay 'a visit to Lady Periam', as the facilities are built on the site of an older building donated by a benefactor of the same name. Similarly in Brasenose College they are known as 'the Longs' as they were built using funds donated by a Lady Long.

In Cambridge, students of Trinity College ask 'Where's the rush matting?' if they want to relieve themselves (presumably the Trinity scholars of anti- quity used to go on the floor), while a visit to the toilets of Christ's College is known as 'keeping a fourth'. This may be explained in three possible ways: firstly the toilets were in the fourth quad; secondly, visiting the toilets was the fourth thing you do in the morning (after going to church, eating breakfast, and smoking a pipe); thirdly the toilets were found on the fourth stair- case.

A Crapper's Glossary

BIDET
This is also the word for a small horse or pony in France; the connection is obvious when you consider that a bidet and a horse are straddled in the same way.

BOG

This English slang term for a toilet is derived from nature's own cesspit. A bog is made up of dangerously unstable marshy ground formed from slowly decomposing vegetable matter. The word is an abbreviation of the 16th century boggard and is related to the Gaelic *bogach* meaning 'soft'.

CACK, CACA

These are derived from the Latin word for excrement, cacare. 'Kakker-boosah' is an obscure 19th- century English slang phrase meaning 'to prematurely void excrement'.

CLOAKROOM

It has been assumed by many that a 'cloakroom' was so called because some medieval privies had a double function, serving as wardrobes as well as toilets. However it is actually derived from *cloacae* the Latin for 'sewer', probably entering the English language via the old French, *cloque*.

CRAP

This word seems to have been popularised by Thomas Crapper, the prominent Victorian plumber whose name appeared on many of his water closets. However the word crap did not originate with Crapper; it first appears in Middle English as *crappe* meaning 'chaff' and is probably related to the old Dutch word *krappen* meaning to 'tear off'. In this latter sense it is very similar in meaning to shit and turd which are both derived from words meaning 'to separate from the body'. The fact that Mr Crapper was so aptly named was simply one of life's happy accidents.

GONGFERMOR
This medieval name for an emptier of cesspits is derived from *gang*, meaning to 'go off' (as in gangrene) and *fermor*, meaning to scour.

JAKES
This is Elizabethan slang and seems to be an abbreviation of 'Jack's House' or 'Jack's Place'.

JOHN
As in 'Jakes' this might be an abbreviation of 'John's House/Place'.

LAVATORY, LATRINE
These words are descended from the Italian *laver* meaning to wash and are related to lather. In the past lavatory could describe a basin, laundry room, bath etc. Today hand-basins are still technically known as lavatories in the bathroom fittings trade, a toilet bowl being known as a closet. It's thought that the confusion came about as a result of the labelling on train doors. Originally the facilities on trains comprised two compartments: a lavatory containing a hand-basin, and

water closet containing a toilet – when the two rooms were combined into one it was simply labelled 'Lavatory' rather than 'Lavatory and WC'. Medieval monks called a wash-house the *lavatorium* and the privy the *necessarium*, hence the phrase 'necessary house' or 'house of necessity'.

Loo

This is either derived from *l'eau* meaning 'water' or *lieu* meaning 'place'. '*Regardez l'eau!*' ('Watch out for the water!') was a warning cry to alert people that a chamber pot was about to be emptied out of a window, while *lieu d'aisance* ('place of comfort') was a French term for the toilet. Some have suggested the word is derived from the name for a female chamber pot, *bordaloue* (*see* Chamber Pots, p. 81).

Nettie

A name for the toilet used in the northeast of England that seems to be a relic from the Roman occupation, the Italian name for a row of toilets being *gabinetti*.

Poo

Poo seems to have been derived from poop a word that referred to the rear of a ship (hence the name 'poop deck'), and which came to be associated with the human rear. In the 18th century it meant to 'break wind', only becoming a term for excrement and defecation in the late 19th century.

PRIVY
A 'private place', derived from the Latin *privatus*.

SHIT
The word 'shit' has been around a long time but was only allowed entry in to the American dictionary as recently as 1961. It is derived from the word *shitten*, itself coming from the old German *skit* meaning to 'separate from the body'. This has given rise to many other similar words, for example the German *scheissen*, Dutch *schijten*, Swedish *skita*, and Danish *skide*.

STOOL
This medical term for a turd is derived from the 'close-stool' the chair-like potty used for centuries. A 'stool sample' is a sample you'd obtain by using a close-stool.

TURD
Like shit this also came from an old Germanic word meaning to 'separate from the body', in this case, *turdam*.

When Toilets Attack

ALL sorts of creatures find their way up to the toilet. Rats have no trouble in navigating the 'soil pipe' (leading from your toilet to the sewer) because, apart from the water in the S-bend, the pipes are dry. Consequently, many people have found sewer rats popping out of their toilets for a breath of fresh air. In rural areas toilets are often home to squirrels, snakes, spiders, and other creatures, some of which have been known to attack when least expected! Composting toilets, where there's no flush to wash unwelcome visitors away, are a particularly favoured hangout for wildlife. An additional attraction is that the composting sewage makes them nice and warm.

CITY sewers also have wildlife problems. Apart from rats, many exotic pets find themselves in the toilet, some from choice. In 1992 a Canadian man was charged with cruelty to animals after his neighbours accused him of flushing his pet python down the loo. In a courtroom re-enactment it was shown that the (rescued) python was irresistibly drawn to the loo and would slither down it of its own accord.

THE most infamous sewer dwellers are alligators. Stories of alligators living in the sewers of New York seem to have started in over-imaginative newspaper reports of the 1930s. Oddly enough these tales are very similar to stories of large ferocious black pigs that were said to inhabit the sewers of Victorian London. Needless to say all these tales have to be taken with a pinch of salt.

REFERENCES

Toilets in History, Elizabeth Newbury, 1999
Flushed With Pride, Wallace Reyburn, 1989
The Complete Loo, Roger Kilroy, 1984
The Water Closet, Roy Palmer, 1973
Thunder, Flush and Thomas Crapper, Adam Hart-Davis, 1997
The Porcelain God, Julie L. Horan, 1996
Merde, Ralph A. Lewin, 1999
Scatalogical Rites of all Nations, Capt. J. G. Bourke, 1891
Dictionary of Word Origins, John Ayto, 1990
The Great Stink of London, Stephen Halliday, 1999
Up the Cistern, James Riddle, 1985
Clean and Decent, Lawrence Wright, 1966
Sewage Solution, Nick Grant et al, 1996
Shell Book of Firsts, Patrick Robertson, 1975
The Gentleman's Magazine February, 1731. Vol 1
The History of Shit, Dominique Laporte, 1993
The Mammoth Book of Oddities, Frank O'Neil, 1996
The Encyclopedia of Unusual Sexual Practises, Brenda Love,
    1995

INDEX

Adamson, Joseph 20
Africa 164–5
    customs and superstitions
    195–6, 201–2
    euphemisms 238
air filters 39
aircraft toilets 130–4, 149–51
Ajax toilet 16
Albert, Prince 56
America 30–33
    cesspits 116
    railway toilets 128
animal fodder 178–9
animals
    eating excrement 211–12
    in toilets 251
Armitage 26
Armitage Shanks 35
army toilets 139–48
Arts, the 223–34
Ashwell, Arthur 105
Australia
    customs and superstitions
    196–7
Automatic toilets 105–6

Baker, Laurence 221
beauty treatments 177
Bennett, Arnold 56
Bible, The
    eating excrement 210
    and sanitation 184–5
    toilets in 140, 190–91
bidets 70–71, 246
    warm-water 38
bioloos 122–3
boats, toilets on 134–7
bourdaloues 86
bowel health 58–60
Bramah, Joseph 18
Brener, Alexander 224
British Patent Perforated Paper
    Company 74
Buddhists 190
Bukowski, Charles 226
Burgess, Anthony 226
Burton, Richard (explorer) 189

'Cat Holes' 140
cesspits 15, 113–17
    deaths in 220
chamber pots 81–90

cheese making 180
chemical toilets 109
    on military aircraft 149
China
customs and superstitions 199
    euphemisms 239
    excrement as fertiliser 171–2
    piss-pillows 83
    punishment 175
    rocket making 178
    toilets in 2, 159–61
cholera 57
Christians 190–2
Churchill, Winston 79
cleaning, household 180
cleaning after crapping 69–78
Cloaca Maxima 4–5
close-stools 87
clysters 59–60
Cohen, Alexander 76–7
cold weather crapping 63–7
colon 47–8
colonic irrigation 60
Commission of Sewers 10
commodes, cosmic 154–7
communal toilets
    in America 32
    in China 160
    medieval 6, 7, 8
    Roman 4
    troughs 21
composting crap 122–5
composting toilets 137
    on ships 147
Considerate Seat 41
constipation 48–50, 61
coprophagy 210–12
cottaging 207–8
crap, composition of 44–7

Crapper, Thomas 20, 26
    flush testing 29
    royal approval 27
Crawford, Joan 203
Cumming, Alexander 17–18
customs 195–203

Dalai Lama 190
death on the loo 215–21
diarrhoea 48–9
diseases from toilets 55–7
door locks 105
Doultons 26, 28
dryers 39
dual flush toilets 37
Duchamp, Marcel 224
Ducketts 26

earth closets 124–5
eating crap
    animals 63–4
    humans 210–12
Edward Johns company 28
Egypt 3
    customs and superstitions 200
    euphemisms 238
elevating seats 37
encopresis 213
enemas 59–60
Eskimos 63–4
    coprophagy 210
    urine shampoo 177
euphemisms 237–44
Europe
    toilets in 166–9

Faecal Containment System
    (FCS) 153–4
fertiliser from excrement 171–4

festivals, toilets at 110
fighter pilots 150–1
films, toilets in the 229–31
Fitzalwyn, Henry 113
flushing
    dual flush toilets 37
    low-flush toilets 36
    power-flush toilets 36
    siphonic flush 20
    in Switzerland 168
    testing 28–9
'flute' toilets 145
Follow-on Latrines (FOL's)
    144–5
France 10, 14, 90
    bidets 70–1
    bourdaloues 86
    clysters 60
    customs and superstitions 199
    euphemisms 238
    excrement as fertiliser 172
    squat toilets 166
Freud, Sigmund 205
fuel 175–6

Garland, Judy 220
Germany
    customs and superstitions
    197–8
Gielgud, Sir John 207
glossary 246–50
glow-in-the-dark seats 41
Gods and toilets 183–93
Godwin, Michael 220
good luck crap 199–200
graffiti 5, 232–3
Great Exhibition, 1851 25, 103
'Great Frost,' 1785 67
'Great Stink' 16

Greece 2–3
    public toilets 101
grow bags 125
gunpowder 178

haemorrhoids 51
Hampton Court 7
Harington, Sir John 16, 192
Hellyers 26
Henry IV, King of France 13–14
Henry VIII, King of England 7,
    10
    close-stools 87
Herrick, Sir Robert 73
Hindus 186–8
Hogarth, William 13
hookworms 53
hopper closets 21
household cleaning 180
humour 231–4
Humphersons 20, 26

incinerator toilets 40
India
    Hindu rules on defecation
    186–8
    railway toilets 128–9
    toilets in 2, 61, 163–4
Inflammatory Bowel Disease
    (IBD) 51, 54
involuntary defecation 174 see
    also diarrhoea
Ireland
    customs and superstitions 200
Islands, toilets on 165–6

Jackson, E.L. 109
James I, King of England 22
Japan

deaths on the toilet 215–16
toilets in 161–3
Jennings, George 26, 29
public toilets 103–4
Jews 184–5
Johnson, Dr Virginia 206
Joyce, James 227

Kellogg, John Harvey 58–9
Kellogg, William Keith 59

ladies urinals 96–8
Lapland
customs and superstitions 200
latrines, military 142–5
laws concerning loos 10–11
laxative abuse 50
literature, toilet-related 225–9
Longfellow, Henry Wadsworth 33
Louis XIV, King of France 61
close stools 88
low-flush toilets 36
Luther, Martin 191–2

macerating toilets 40
Maddock, Thomas 33
Mallon, Mary 56
Mann, John 20
marketing loos 27–8
Maturing Theatre Latrines (MTL's) 144
medi-loos 39–40
medicine 176–7
medieval 6–11
cesspits 114
customs and superstitions 197–8, 200
public toilets 102

urinals 82
megacolon 50
Meyer, Russ 233
Michael, George 207
mile-high club 208–9
military toilets 139–51
Modular Initial Deployment Latrines (MIDL's) 144
moist paper 77
Moule, Henry 124–5, 174
movies, toilets in the 229–31
Mozart, Wolfgang Amadeus 205–6
Muslims 188–90

Navy, toilets in the 146–8

ornamental chamber pots 83–5
ornamental loos 26–7, 35

pan closets 17
paper 55, 73–8
Peacekeeper, The 40–1
pedestal closets 26–7
'pee bags' 150
Pepys, Samuel 15
personal hygiene 177
phrases 237–51
'piddle packs' 150
pit toilets 163
plug closets 17
Poland
toilet paper 75–6
Portaloos 110, 137
'pot stickers' 168
power-flush toilets 36
practical jokes 233
Presley, Elvis 50, 216
public toilets 101–11

Pujol, Joseph 225
punishment 174–5

Rabelais, François 227–9
railway toilets 127–30
reredorters 7–8
restaurants, toilets in 107
rhyming slang 244–5
Romans 4–5
    chamber pots 81
    customs and superstitions 203
    Gods and toilets 183
    public toilets 101
    wiping 71
roundworms 52–3
royal deaths 216–18
royal souvenirs 193
royal stools 87–9
rude toilet behaviour 205–13
Russia
    euphemisms 238–9
    squat toilets 166
    toilet paper 75–6

Sargon, King 1
Scott Brothers 74
seat-action closets 28
seat covers/cleaners 38
seat warmers 38
seats
    elevating seats 37
    glow-in-the-dark seats 41
self-raising lids 38
septic tanks 116–17
sewage, disposal of 15–16,
        120–5
    aircraft 130–4
    Antarctic 65–6
    chamber pots 89–90

medieval 8–11
    railway trains 129–30
ships and boats 134–7
    treatment of 119–20
sexuality and defecation 205–13
Shanks 26
Sheppard, Alan 153
ships, toilets on 134–7, 146–8
shops, toilets in 107
Simon, John 77
sink toilets 37
siphonic flush 20
sit-down toilets 167–8
slang 239–46
'soak pits' 142
space, toilets in 153–7
Spain 14
    customs and superstitions 202
speakers 39
squat toilets 166
squatting 43–4, 94–5
standing up 63, 94–8
submarines, toilets on 147–8
superstitions 195–203
Sweden
    composting toilets 123–4
Swift, Jonathan 85–6, 103, 108,
        225
Switzerland
    toilet flushing in 168

tanks, lack of toilets in 145–6
tanning 180
tapeworms 53–4
taxes on loos 12
textile industry 179–80
threadworms 53
tipper closets 21–2
tobacco curing 180

toilet demons 196
toilet diseases 55–7
toilet humour 231–4
toilet paper 55, 73–8
toilet roll holders 78
'toilet slaves' 209–10
'toilet targets' 95
transport toilets 127–37
trench latrines 110, 140–1
troughs 21
'Turkish toilets' 166
Twyford, Thomas 19, 27
'toilet targets' 95
typhoid 56–7

upgrading 39
urinals 82, 93–9
    military 142
    in space 155
Utilidor system 65
UV lamps 39

'Vacant/Engaged' door locks 105
vacuum toilets 37, 131–2, 136–7
    on ships 147
Velez, Lupe 219
Victorians
    bidets 71
    earth closets 125
    excrement as fertilisers 172–3
    public toilets 103–5
    toilet development 15–16,
    19–22, 25–9
    toilet paper 74
    toilet rhymes 229
Vinci, Leonardo da 13, 234
voyeurs 206–7

warfare 178

wash-down closets 19–20, 167
wash-out closets 19, 167–8
washers 69–71
Waugh, Evelyn 219, 225–6
Wheeler, Seth 74
Whittington, Dick 108
wipers 71–8
words and phrases 237–51
Wyngarde, Peter 207

'Zimbabwe long drop' 165